FUN WITH SATAN

A Raucous Debate About
The Devil's Identity

Kaufman & Stack

ALSO BY CHRIS & DANTE

<u>Chris Kaufman</u>

Kingdom Over Empire: Following Jesus In the American Empire

<u>Dante Stack</u>

Non-Fiction

Fun with Gilgamesh
Fun with Jesus
Fun with the Apocrypha

Fiction

Solve the World (Volumes I-IV)
Man Against Fate

TABLE OF CONTENTS

What this Book Is

Introduction

I. A Horned, Red Devil?

II. The Serpent?

III. The Antichrist?

IV. The Nothing?

V. Azazel?

VI. Mammon?

VII. Chemosh?

VIII. Lilith?

IX. Death?

X. The Prince of Rome?

XI. The Winner?

XII. God?

XIII. Who is Satan?

Addendum A: Demons

Addendum B: Money

WHAT THIS BOOK IS

Will the real Satan please stand up? Please stand up. Please stand up.

What we've got here is a conversation between two Christians who are honestly trying to figure out who the hell Satan is. Debate has been chosen as the most appropriate format to organize our ongoing conversation. Within these pages, you'll find our attempts at humor awkward, strained, and sometimes repugnant. Sorry about that. The topic of Satan, especially among Christians, comes with armfuls of assumptions and baggage, but rarely much analysis. What follows is a sincere (albeit often trite) effort to bring the angel of darkness out into the light. In attempting to do so, we don't take ourselves too seriously. We trust that the one who is against us is no match for the one who is for us.

We've formatted the book into 13 chapters (plus an introduction and a couple of addendums). Each chapter explores a specific question about Satan's possible identity. It's kinda like that game *Guess Who?*, but with the Devil instead of all those white, middle-class people. Every chapter, Dante will try to convince you that Satan is a specific idea or person (such as the Antichrist, or the Moabite deity Chemosh), and Chris will do his darndest to break that argument into smithereens. Generally, the chapters begin with opening statements. Volleys of rebuttals from both sides follow. In the last chapter, Dante and Chris offer their last, heartfelt hypotheses as to who the Satan of the Bible really is. Chapter by chapter, it's up to you to decipher who makes the stronger argument. Good luck with that.

So, are you ready to *Guess Who?*

Meet Dante

Hey there, I'm the fella playing the role of devil's advocate. Every chapter, I'll come at you swinging for the fences, trying to convince you that I've got Satan's identity down pat. I'll be taking the affirmative approach: Satan is this! And when that gets shut down: Satan is that! I like writing with staccato sentences, referencing Ancient Near East culture, and talking too much about anteaters. Yup. That's me. I'm sure we'll be fast friends.

Meet Chris

Heidy-Ho, good neighbor! I'm Chris, Dante's buzzkill. Think of me as the red right hand on the metaphorical leash, reigning in Dante's big swings when he gets carried away. I'm coming to each table with a healthy dose of skepticism about the devil's identity. When it feels like chaos is on all sides, I'll be the rational voice calling you out of the Satanic rabbit-holes you might fall down. Don't worry, I will give you plenty of pop-culture references and early church quotes to make sense of this mess you've found yourself in.

INTRODUCTION

Dante's Position: You Shouldn't Read this Book
The best book ever written is *The Monster at the End of this Book: Starring Lovable, Furry Old Grover*. There's no battle here. It surpasses the existential dread of Kafka, flies higher than any lyric of Bob Dylan, and hits its ending stronger than Romeo and Juliet's tragic suicide. You think something else is better? Fight me.

Let's review that great muppet masterpiece.

It begins with horrid self-realization. Grover, the cute Sesame Street muppet serving as narrator, has discovered something grotesque: the end of his own book includes a monster. This terrifies the little critter. Grover's reality confines him to the pages of the book. There is no escape. Page one of Grover's odyssey echoes the words on the gates of Dante's *Inferno*:

Abandon all hope ye who enter here.

Ironically, we can't help but do the very thing that Dante Alighieri forbids. We hope.

A bitter irony descends on Grover. It's a deep realization that lies just beyond the words on the page. Grover knows it. He doesn't spell it out for us. Of course not. This is a kid's book. Kids are smart. Why would Jesus tell us to enter the kingdom of heaven like children? Kids are smarter than us. What's the real existential terror that Grover knows in his heart of hearts?

It's you.

You are the monster. You are the monster because you keep turning the page. If you never get to the end of the book, then Grover never has to face his predestined fate. You have all the power. Grover begs, he pleads, he does everything in his power to stop you from turning the page. This is the Milgram experiment. You remember that one; where people electrocuted other folks for not answering questions correctly, thus proving how evil social contagions like Nazism infect society. That one. That's this. We are torturing Grover with every page turn. We torture him. And we like it.

Grover knows it. Deep in the recesses of his furry little heart, he knows it. We feed off his trauma. We are the Mr. Hydes of *Monsters Inc,* feeding off the screams of the innocent.

Then the end comes. As we arrive at that denouement, Grover states the obvious. There's nothing there. Don't be fooled. His words betray him. He tells us that he must be the monster. His logic sounds fair at first. He's the only one on the page. The monster must be him.

It's not. He knows it. But he'll never tell us the truth.
No, he'll never reveal the awful revelation to us. Not us.

Abandon all hope, ye who enter here.

> *Keep on hearing, but do not understand;*
> *Keep on seeing, but do not perceive.*
> *Make the heart of this people dull,*
> *And their eyes heavy,*
> *And blind their eyes;*
> *Lest they see with their eyes,*
> *And hear with their ears,*
> *And understand with their hearts,*
> *And turn and be healed.*
> Isaiah 6:9-10 ESV

> *Then I said, "IIow long, O Lord?"*
> Isaiah 6:11a ESV

Are you having fun yet?

Chris's Position: You Have to Read this Book

The search for Satan might seem like a silly one; maybe even dangerous. Why look for the monster at the end of the book? Why seek out evil? As a pastor, my advice for congregant members is to pursue God, to cling to the *good* of this world. It may seem like an odd endeavor for us to try and find the monster.

My dog Chance has developed an irritating habit. If he needs to go outside, he has learned that sitting in front of my tv is the best way to get my attention. Often, I'm enthralled in the sitcom I'm watching and don't want to get up and go on a 20-minute potty break adventure with him. Eventually, he'll figure out that I'm ignoring him and position his body to block more of the screen. If I continue to ignore him and he can't take up any more space, he'll get vocal. He starts with soft, high pitch whines that inevitably devolve into loud whoofs. After a while, he'll get fed up and throw the full force of his body at me to get me off the couch. At this point, I have to get up or he'll start destroying the house.

Ignoring the 65-pound beast in the room will always make the problem worse. Eventually, he starts ripping up the furniture and peeing on the rugs. To deal with the situation, though, you have to know who the beast is.

C.S. Lewis, the famed *Narnia* writer, once said, "There are two equal and opposite errors into which our race can fall about devils. One is to disbelieve in their existence. The other is to believe, and to feel excessive and unhealthy interest in them."

The danger is to misunderstand Lewis here. So often, this is cited as a reason not to talk about the devil; to ignore the beast. But this can't possibly be Lewis' expectation. For goodness sake, he wrote *The Screwtape Letters,* a book focused on demonic letter correspondence. Lewis knew there is a line between healthy understanding and obsession. This journey we're embarking on is not meant to add to the libraries of conspiracy-driven demonologies. Instead, we are seeking honesty and understanding. It has never benefited Christianity to stick our heads in the sand and ignore this problem.

Who is this monster, and why does he have so many different names across the world? Perhaps he is not who you believe he is. There may be something more dark and sinister going on here. It's time to address the beast sitting in front of the tv.

DEBATE I

Is Satan a Horned, Red Devil?

**Dante's Opening Statement: Satan
IS a Horned, Red Devil**
The third chapter of Zechariah presents a set piece that we Westerners can easily envision. Even if you haven't watched one of the myriad iterations of *Law & Order*, you've absorbed the image through osmosis: the courtroom.

You've got four key figures: a judge, a defendant, his defense attorney, and the prosecutor. Zechariah makes it easy to tell who's who. There's the defendant (some dude) standing next to his attorney (an angel) facing the judge (God). Satan is the prosecution. It says it right there.

...and Satan standing at his right hand to accuse him
Zechariah 3:1 ESV

I know we're just beginning, but the Occam's Razor interpretation is the best one: Satan is who we think he is. He's the fusion of an ambulance chaser and Pennywise the Clown.

Satan has always been with us. His presence is felt most distinctly at the beginning and end of the Bible. He's there to tempt Eve in the garden. The whole Biblical drama is set in motion because of him. He sneaks in once in a while in the middle (this Zechariah passage, torturing Job, tempting Jesus) and is center stage in the finale (Revelation).

Think of any good villain in any decent story worth a damn. The villain is alluded to in the beginning, shows up somewhere near the middle for a scene, and is summarily defeated by the hero in the end. *Harry Potter*. Easy. Voldemort shows up at Potter's birth, sprinkles himself into Potter's life throughout his adventures, and then must be defeated at the end of the epic. Pretty much the same thing with Sauron in *Lord of the Rings*. This is how storytelling goes.

Tell me: why shouldn't I believe that Satan is exactly as we imagine him to be?

Chris's Opening Statement: The Red Horned Cartoon Satan is a Myth

On June 10th, 2006, an episode of one of the oldest beloved sci-fi series aired; *Doctor Who*. This episode, however, was unlike anything the writers on the show had tackled before. Before this, *Doctor Who* tended to avoid the mystical and religious, instead opting for time and space travel tales. But here, they were finally going to tackle the origin of all evil in the universe.

The Doctor and his companion stumble their way onto a spaceship attempting to research a black hole. Along the way, they meet the crew and a hive-minded group of aliens called the Ood. While exploring the black hole, the Ood begins to act strange. Our heroes discover that the hive mind is under the influence of some "other" force inside the black hole.

It's then that the force behind the Ood's strange behavior identifies itself as the origin of all evil. In a bone-chilling scene, the hive mind creatures speak in unison, prompting the Doctor to ask, "Which devil are you?"

"All of them," the deep voice echoes through the darkness. He is the truth behind the myth. He was before all time, space, and matter. He is the great monster behind all legends; a figure impossible to a man of science such as the Doctor.

It's a disturbing scene primarily because we cannot see the face of the great beast. He is our worst nightmare, the most twisted and wild of our deepest and darkest fantasies. The episode builds and builds until the moment the Doctor must stand face to face with the old devil.

As the camera pans up…

...the most ridiculous CGI monster ever rendered stands before us. He's the picture-perfect version of the silly red devil, horns and all. The evilest part of his appearance is probably the soul of the director that green-lit this scene. It's laughable.

Honestly though, how do you make our standard picture of the devil scary? He's a guy with horns and a pitchfork, hardly the stuff of nightmares in a culture saturated with movies like *Saw* and *Hereditary*. But certainly, this image of Satan must come from somewhere vital for it to have penetrated the most beloved show in British history.

Enter the artists and poets of the Renaissance. It is here that the creatives seem to have given themselves the task of envisioning the devil. The only problem? Scripture gives us almost no clear description of Satan.

Jesus tells us in John 8 that the devil is the father of lies and a murderer, but we don't get any comment on his appearance. Peter tells us Satan walks around "like a roaring lion", but certainly we aren't to believe he is a literal cat. Maybe the best description we get is found in Revelation.

> *Then another sign appeared in heaven:*
> *it was a great fiery red dragon, with*
> *seven heads and ten horns,*
> *and seven royal crowns on his heads.*

> *His tail swept down a third of heaven's stars*
> *and threw them to the earth.*
> *The dragon stood in front of the woman*
> *who was about to give birth*
> *so that when she gave birth, he*
> *might devour her child.*
> Revelation 12:3-4 CEB

But is this to be taken literally? John sounds like a toddler asked to describe the most fantastic monster he can conceive. Indeed, Revelation is steeped in thick metaphors. If John did mean it literally, the church would have picked up on this, and we would see more images of Satan as a giant dragon.

Given this description, the Renaissance artists seemed to take inspiration for the devil from places outside of Scripture. They used bits and pieces from pagan gods to fill in the gaps Scripture leaves. Horns and goat legs and mighty pitchforks all appear in depictions of various near-eastern deities. These artists used syncretized versions of Satan to show where all the false "gods" originated.

But there is one obscure reference these artists overlooked. In Ezekiel 28, we get a comparison of an earthly king to our wicked devil.

> *You were full of wisdom and beauty,*
> *the image of perfection.*
> *You were in Eden, God's garden.*

You were covered with gold and every precious stone:
carnelian, topaz, and moonstone;
beryl, onyx, and jasper;
lapis lazuli, turquoise, and emerald.
On the day that you were created,
finely crafted pendants and
engravings were prepared.
You, a winged creature, were installed as a guardian.
I placed you in God's holy mountain where
you walked among the stones of fire.
From the day you were created until
injustice was found in you,
your ways were assured.
Ezekiel 28:12-15 CEB

God tells us He created Satan as a *cherub*, you know, another word for angel. Ezekiel shows the devil as being beautiful, ornate even. Given what we know about the looks of other angels described, I'm sure Satan would look weird to us, but definitely not the ram-horned monster with a goatee we've all grown up believing.

To add to our evidence, we have an image of Satan from long before our Renaissance friends got a hold of the idea. In the Basilica of Sant'apollinare Nuovo in Ravenna, Italy, exists a sixth-century mosaic of Jesus. On his left, guarding the sheep of the church, is a red angel. It's sort of a strange image to us today, but to the early church red symbolized the Kingdom of God, bought with the blood of Christ. On his right, stand the goats representing the souls of the damned. Guarding them is another angel, this time blue. This radiant figure is thought to be the first depiction of Satan by the early church. Missing are the horns and hooves of a much later era.

Once the Doctor has the curtain pulled back and the big bad CGI Satan is revealed, David Tennet says something rather interesting.

"I accept that you exist. I don't have to accept what you are, but your physical existence, I give you that."

The same is true for us today. We can accept the existence of the Satan figure. But evidence from the early church and the Bible shows us that we don't have to buy into the idea of a silly red-horned devil. We'd be fools to. There is an adversary here, but we don't have to accept the clunky CGI facade.

Dante's Rebuttal: Horns Have Meaning
You used European art to make your point, so I'll do the same. If it wasn't for the Sistine Chapel, history might very well remember the artist Michelangelo for his sculptures rather than his paintings. The creators of *Teenage Mutant Ninja Turtles* clearly understood this. T he turtle who bears the artist's name, Michelangelo, gets two swords as his weapon of choice. The swords represent the blades that carve images out of stone. See? It's so obvious.

When Michelangelo was tasked with carving the prophet Moses out of marble, he made what many saw as an extremely peculiar choice. He gave Moses two horns.

Now, Mikey wasn't merely taking an extreme artist's liberty providing Moses some personal antennae. He was reading his Bible. Apparently, the ancient Hebrew word for 'rays' and 'horns' are interchangeable. After Moses encountered God on Mount Sinai, our English translations of the Bible state that Moe's face shone like the heavens. He had rays of sunshine beaming off his facade. When St. Jerome created the standard Latin version of the Bible, instead of beams of light, Jerome understood the Hebrew to be saying that encountering God caused spontaneous horn generation. Thus, Michelangelo's Moses has horns.

Having horns is an analogy for having been in the presence of God. If Satan was chief among all of God's angels, then he would have been closest to God's actual presence, right? So then, it's quite likely he has horns. Maybe two. Or maybe ten, like this Revelation passage EXPLICITLY states:

> *And I saw a beast rising out of the sea,*
> *with ten horns and seven heads,*
> *with ten diadems on its horns and*
> *blasphemous names on its heads.*
> Revelation 13:1 ESV

Chris's Rebuttal: Horns Have Meaning, But Not The Meaning Your Thinking Of

So, old Moe is a little horny, huh? Sorry, I couldn't resist.

In all seriousness, though, that's a pretty solid point. There is precedent for the Hebrew word *qaran* meaning "to have horns". However, that particular version of the word only appears four times throughout the Old Testament and in all but one, we understand it to mean "horns" in a figurative sense. Believe it or not, this Hebrew word has an older brother, *qeren*, which appears 76 times and always translates as literal horns. So had the writer wanted to convey literal horns on Moses' head, he had the vernacular to do so and yet didn't.

We can speculate all day whether *qaran* should be taken literally or figuratively. We could also argue about whether we should take St. Jerome's Latin Vulgate as an accurate translation, given that when we read it, we are translating a text that has already been translated, which can start to feel like a frustrating game of telephone. For me, though, I think the most exciting conversation is around Michelangelo.

Michelangelo had an interesting way of coming up with designs for the faces of his Biblical characters. Since no one knew what Moses or David looked like, Mike would sculpt their faces after people he knew. The statue of Moses was commissioned for Pope Julius II's tomb, so it should be no surprise that Mikey would sculpt Moses' face as that of the Pope.

What ended up being the tomb and statues was not the original plan. Michelangelo had planned on 40 sculptures with figures such as St. Paul, but the Pope interrupted Mike's work, much to his dismay, and considerably downsized the project. After all this, Michelangelo finished the statue with the Pope's face. By all the evidence we have available, Michelangelo wasn't the Pope's biggest fan. The Sistine Chapel was only created after the Pope forced Mikey to do it begrudgingly. Mike was a sculptor, not a painter, and it frustrated him greatly to be forced into using a medium he wasn't familiar with.

Between the forced panting and interruptions to his original vision, Michelangelo had every reason to dislike the Pope. Hold that thought for a moment.

Mike seemed to have beef with another group of people too. Scholars like Giovanni Careri and Barbara Wisch have noted that Michelangelo, though not a devout Catholic, was influenced by the anti-Semitism that was rampant in the Renaissance era. They, and others, have pointed out the painter's use of a literal yellow badge in the

Sistine Chapel paintings to identify Jews within his artwork.

Of one figure, Wisch notes in *Redressing Jews on Michelangelo's Sistine Ceiling*:

> "The badge stitched a constructed Otherness — negative stereotypes of Jewishness — into the very fabric of [the figure's] being. He portrayed with a grimacing expression, which had become a visual topos of Jewishness. He sits with hands crossed between his legs, evoking a bound barbarian captive from Roman triumphal monuments... He is the only male figure on the ceiling to wear earrings... European men at this time did not adorn themselves in this manner. A pierced ear also marked a Hebrew slave who refused freedom, preferring to serve his master forever."

If nothing else, these inclusions seem to be evidence that Michelangelo wasn't immune to the negative stereotypes of his day. It's probably a good thing the *Teenage Mutant Ninja Turtles* left the anti-Semitism out of Michelangelo's character traits.

What does this have to do with Michelangelo's Moses statue? In his book *The Antisemitic Origin of Michelangelo's Horned Moses*, Dr. Stephen Bertman argues that the horns added to Moses don't stem from St. Jerome's mistranslation, but rather a purposeful inclusion on the face of a man Michelangelo hated. "By endowing Moses with horns, Michelangelo not only mocked the giver of the Ten Commandments but also satirized his nemesis Pope Julius II", states Bertman. Jews as devils were a common trope during the Renaissance, so was Michelangelo reading his Bible, or did he have more sinister motives? It seems the former is more likely.

The final nail in the coffin on this is the idea that Satan would be a horned being because he was close to God. If that were the case, we would expect all those who came into contact with God to have horns. While several other figures in the Old Testament have passing encounters with God without growing horns, the most prominent comes to us from the New Testament.

During His time on Earth, Jesus takes his disciples up to a mountain. It's here that the scene known as The Transfiguration occurs. While the disciples are standing there, Moses and Elijah appear next to Jesus. But here's the crucial part of the story:

> *He was transformed in front of them.*
> *His face shone like the sun, and his*
> *clothes became as white as light.*
> Matthew 17:2 CEB

The disciples witness an event meant to call back to the moment Moses met with God, and Jesus' face "shone like the sun." No horns, just light.

Logically, if those in the presence of God grow horns, then we should see St. Jerome's Vulgate translate this event as he did for Moses in Exodus. But, instead, we don't. Jerome sees Jesus as shining like the sun too.

Here's the crazy thing, though. If we understand these verses to tell us that those in the presence of God physically change into bright glowing figures, then it helps us make sense of the Bible's description of Satan:

> *How you've fallen from heaven,*
> *morning star, son of dawn!*
> *You are cut down to earth,*
> *helpless on your back!*
> Isaiah 14:12 CEB

Satan is called the morning star and the son of the dawn. In Hebrew, this means "bright glowing one". As you mentioned, if Satan was the closest being to God, it stands to reason that he would be a bright glowing figure instead of one with horns, and that's precisely what we see!

At the end of the day, Satan cannot be a cartoonish CGI monster because Scripture gives us exactly what he looks like. He is a being who spent time in the presence of God, and he retained his glow to show it.

DEBATE II

Is Satan the Serpent?

Dante's Opening Statement:
Satan is Eden's Serpent

I love animals. Anteaters! What's their deal? Have you seen the tongues on those suckers? Insanity! I'm pretty sure the Manhattan Project boys must have accidentally turned their beta rays at a Dr. Seuss drawing, and that's the real reason anteaters exist. They defy explanation. I love them so.

Cuttlefish can do this crazy hypnotism thing. Their skin turns into a strobe light to bewilder their prey. It's essentially what the Batman villain, Penguin, does when he spins his umbrella. Except cuttlefish are real! I love them so.

Camels are ridiculous. Yes, I'd like two humps of sugar in my coffee. But tomorrow, I need to cut back. Just one hump. I love them so.

I love them all: all of God's good creatures.

Except snakes.

It's just… everything about them. Good, God-loving animals walk. Or swim. Or fly. Or crawl. Snakes don't do any of that. They slither. Gross. Listen to this description, from dkfindout.com, of what slithering is: "Most snakes glide forward by using their ribs and belly scales to push backward, first on one side and then the other." Eww.

My unbeatable logic can be refined simply into this compact syllogism.
Satan is gross. If something is gross, it makes you go "eww." Snakes make me go "eww." Therefore, Satan is a snake. I'm just presenting facts here.

The Bible says so.

Chris's Opening Statement: Satan is Not a Physical Snake

For the first time, Dante, I think you and I can agree on something! Snakes are gross. They are one of the few animals that ruin everything. It's never a good idea to bring a snake anywhere.

My first exposure to the idea of snakes was a story my father used to tell when I was young. See, when he was a kid, his older brother worked at a zoo. One day when it was his turn for show and tell, he got to have his brother bring in one of the zoo's snakes. My dad's brother brought in a 14-foot anaconda to show off. Bringing a snake to a 5th graders classroom is a terrible idea. I don't know what went wrong, but somehow the snake got spooked and started wrapping itself around my uncle. It was a whole thing. They called the police, but thankfully they got the snake off of him. Snakes ruin everything.

But does that fact make them intrinsically evil? Or worse, the *father* of all evil? It's a substantial logical leap from "snakes are gross" to "snakes are evil incarnate." So, as my math teachers were fond of saying: show your work! Where does the Bible "say so"?

Dante's Rebuttal: The Bible Explicitly Says that Satan is the Serpent

Easy.

> *And he seized the dragon, that ancient serpent,*
> *who is the devil and Satan,*
> *and bound him for a thousand years…*
> Revelation 20:2 ESV

The text explicitly connects the snake of Genesis to the identity of Satan.

Satan is a snake.

Chris's Rebuttal: Revelation's Retcon

Alright, Mr. Film Nerd, riddle me this... Who shot first? Greedo or Han? Depending on who you ask, this question can be pretty controversial.

In the original release of *Star Wars: A New Hope,* fans watched as the bad boy Harrison Ford shot a rival bounty hunter named Greedo in cold blood. Upon later releases of the movie, director and creator George Lucas changed this scene to show a blaster bolt leaving Greedo's gun first. Lucas made the change because he wanted the audience to sympathize with Han which is a little hard to do if your hero kills in cold blood. Changing a piece of work to reflect a different meaning is a practice called retconning, and George got super familiar with it in his first three movies. The *Star Wars* we watch today on Disney+ has had scenes altered extensively to give us the story we now know. Disney is far from the first group to practice retconning, though.

We know that Revelation is written several thousand years after the composition of Genesis. I don't believe you will raise any objection to me stating that the writer of Revelation is attempting to communicate a different message than the author of the Genesis account. That's not a bad thing, but it does mean that the temptation exists to retcon meaning, events, and even characters.

To be fair, Genesis is pretty vague when it comes to depicting who the snake was. The only description we get of this thing is that it was,

> *the most intelligent of all the wild animals*
> *that the Lord God had made.*
> Genesis 3:1 CEB

Also, this crafty little guy can talk, how cute, right?

Unfortunately, the only other info we get on it is when God curses it:

> *Because you did this,*
> *you are the one cursed*
> *out of all the farm animals,*
> *out of all the wild animals.*
> *On your belly you will crawl,*
> *and dust you will eat*
> *every day of your life.*
> Genesis 3:14 CEB

Wait, what? This snake didn't already crawl on his belly? This snake had... legs? Maybe arms? Is Trogdor the Burninator confirmed within the Biblical canon?!?!

Setting my Homestar Runner fantasies aside, this seems like a pretty big idea to gloss over, right? Like, I need some answers on what's happening with this snake's physiology! One thing is evident here, though: the Genesis author thought of his snake as a snake. If Revelation tells us Satan is the snake, it's nothing more than a retcon of the original author's intent.

Dante's Rebuttal: The Past was Weird

Darren Aronofsky's weirdo attempt at telling a version of the Biblical flood story, starring Russell Crowe as the titular *Noah*, was ridiculed by Christians and religious skeptics alike. It somehow found a way to alienate itself from just about everyone. Naturally, I kinda love it.

The flick's take on Noah and his family is super weird and takes some bizarre dramatic turns. What it does showcase, however, is this little idea, over and over again. The idea is plenty simple, but one I think we don't readily accept. That idea: the world used to be different. All our technology and all our tools help us see into the past, sure. But it only sees into a past that is predictable and on a timeline that we can easily link ourselves to.

We can't time travel backwards. We can dig pot shards out of the earth and assemble dino bones, but we can't go back. Granted, we can make educated guesses about what the past looked like, but too often our hubris leads us to unwarranted certainties. We say in our hearts: I know what happened. But we don't know. We can't.

Yes, it sounds goofier than Goofy taking Pluto for a walk, but if the Bible says that the Serpent had legs before the fall, who am I to say otherwise?

Chris's Rebuttal: Revelation's Retcon Doesn't Make Satan A Literal Snake

Life would be better if we could all build a time machine and see the Garden of Eden for ourselves. Unfortunately, this isn't *Back To The Future*, and in the real world, we have to use the best information available to make logical conclusions. The good news is we don't have to fly blind when it comes to interpreting the Scriptures. As my favorite bumbling Apostle likes to say:

*By his divine power,
the Lord has given us everything we
need for life and godliness
through the knowledge of the one who called us
by his own honor and glory.*
2nd Peter 1:3 CEB

If God has given us everything we need for our lives and knowledge, He must provide us with ways to know Satan isn't a literal snake. Enter *The Talmud:* one giant set of volumes comprising close to a thousand years of Jewish thought on the Old Testament. This thing is thick and complicated. Rabbis study it their whole lives, and this thing can leave them puzzled sometimes. The best way to describe attempting to read *The Talmud* is that it's like taking a math test while many people (all smarter than you) scream at the top of their lungs.

Even though *The Talmud* is loud and complicated, it can often offer us a better understanding of how the Jews have interpreted these Scriptures. These discussions in *The Talmud*, called Germias, consist of several rabbis arguing various points back and forth. For example, while arguing over different types of meats, the rabbis provide a keen insight into common Jewish thought about the serpent in the Garden:

"Rabbi Yehuda ben Teima would say: 'Adam,

> the first man, would dine in the Garden of Eden, and the ministering angels would roast meat for him and strain wine for him. The snake glanced at him and saw his glory, and was jealous of him, and for that reason the snake incited him to sin and caused his banishment from the Garden.'"
> (Sanhedrin 59b)

This shows us that some of the greatest Jewish rabbis believed the snake in the Garden was just that; a regular, run of the mill, natural snake that got jealous of the food Adam ate and so incited him to sin. Satan being this snake isn't raised here because the idea of Satan doesn't enter Jewish thought until hundreds of years after the composition of Genesis.

It's also worth noting that the retcon of Satan in the popular zeitgeist doesn't fall in line with modern Jewish thought either. In seeking to answer the very question we are, Rabbi David Rosenfeld says, "The Serpent was a physical animal which was part of the natural world." This isn't a point of debate anymore; it's a fact. The writer of Genesis didn't intend for us to see Satan behind this snake.

I doubt you'd argue that *Gilgamesh* is the oldest story known to man. I don't need to tell you that within the *Gilgamesh* narrative is another snake. This snake snatches away the plant of life that our hero Gilgamesh is seeking. The plant heals the snake instead of Gilgamesh. Now it's not beat for beat, but the basic principles remain the same, just reversed. Our heroes presumably have life never-ending, and along comes a crafty snake that helps to snatch that life away from them.

Let's say the author of Genesis knew of the *Gilgamesh* tale. It would make a lot of sense for him to borrow the villain of such a well-known story. We also know that other cultures around the Hebrews worshiped snakes as deities, like the Egyptians. So why not use a natural snake as the trickster responsible for bringing evil into the world?

All this leaves us with a few questions, though. First, why did I grow up in Sunday School hearing how Satan tricked Adam and Eve to eat the fruit? Second, which author is correct, the original or the one who retcons? Who freaking shot first?!?!

The only way to reconcile all of these competing truths isn't all that complicated. Satan is not literally a snake.

Sure, Revelation tells us that Satan is an "ancient serpent," but keep in mind that Revelation speaks heavily in metaphor throughout its narrative. By the time the Revelator comes on the scene, snakes are associated with the worship of false gods. Furthermore, they are evil creatures that bite God's chosen people… (*cough* Paul *cough*). Snakes are gross representations of evil, so why not retcon Satan as the same snake who deceived the first couple? If the author of Genesis could borrow their villain, why not borrow it again? But it is not a literal retcon; the author is not proposing that Satan is literally a snake. Instead, he paints Satan as the thing snakes have come to embody within his culture, evil.

DEBATE III

Is Satan the Antichrist?

Dante's Opening Statement: Satan is the Antichrist, duh!

I mean, I don't know what we're doing here if Satan isn't the dude whose main function is to be the Anti-Jesus.

Chris's Opening Statement: The Antichrist Isn't Any One Person

Let's just cut to the chase here, no clever one-liners or grandiose metaphors. The Antichrist isn't Satan because the Antichrist isn't any one person. Heck, as Biblically understood, the Antichrist isn't any person really; it's an action.

The church is all over the map on this one historically, but looking at Scripture reveals precisely who the Antichrist is, and it's not even the Scripture you're probably thinking. In the back of everyone's New Testament sit two small letters; 1st and 2nd John. (3rd John is there too, but it's not essential to our discussion, so like virtually every other preacher, I'm going to ignore its existence).

Quite plainly, 1st and 2nd John are letters to various groups of believers dealing with a myriad of issues. One of the big ones was false teachers telling the church that Jesus wasn't the Messiah. As a result, John has a pretty pointed thing to say about them:

> *Who is the liar?*
> *Isn't it the person who denies that Jesus is the Christ?*
> *This person is the antichrist: the one who*
> *denies the Father and the Son.*
> 1st John 2:22 CEB

See, John says that the Antichrist is a person who denies that Jesus is the Christ. But, of course, John is talking about human teachers spewing heresy, so don't even come at me with that 'But Satan is the *father* of lies!' nonsense.

The only other appearance of this term comes in John's second letter:

> *Many deceivers have gone into the world*
> *who do not confess that Jesus Christ*
> *came as a human being.*
> *This kind of person is the deceiver and the antichrist.*
> 2nd John 1:7 CEB

John is the first heresy hunter, and he's kicking butt and taking names. Human names. Not devilish ones. Pop culture and goofball series like *Left Behind* have drastically warped what the Scripture claims clear as day. Satan isn't the Antichrist anymore than you are, Dante, because you would never deny Jesus is the Messiah.

> *Even the demons believe this, and*
> *they tremble with fear.*
> James 2:19 CEB

It's an open and shut case. Hallelujah, amen, you are dismissed.

Dante's Rebuttal: An Objection and an Inquiry
But Satan is the Father of lies!

A question for you, old chap, has the Day of the Lord come yet?

Chris's Response: Fine, Sustained.
Yes and no. It all depends on what you are really trying to ask me under your veiled ruse. So, state your case!

Dante's Rebuttal: Look at the Letters to the Thessalonians
The Day of the Lord is prophesied about heavily in the Old Testament. It brings with it great wrath from God (Joel 2:1-2; Amos 5:18-20; Zech 1:14-15), as well as divine blessing (Isa 4:2-6; 30:26; Hos 2:18-23; Joel 3:9-21; Amos 9:11-15; Mic 4:6-8; Zeph 2:7; Zech 14:6-9). Some passages make it sound as if the Day of the Lord is not a singular event, but happens whenever a kingdom (e.g. Assyrians,

Babylonians, Edomites) is humbled. Yet despite those allusions, there are other passages, such as Joel 3, which sound as if the only thing that could fulfill the prophecy and be the titular 'Day of the Lord' is the end of the world as we know it.

If you were to read just the OT and the four Gospels, you might be tempted to say the Day of the Lord is Christ's resurrection (or perhaps the crucifixion itself). The prophecies for this future event, however, continue throughout the New Testament. Paul alludes to the coming Day of the Lord in multiple letters. Perhaps his most oft-quoted line comes in 1st Thessalonians:

> *For you yourselves are fully aware that*
> *the day of the Lord will come like a thief in the night.*
> 1 Thessalonians 5:2 ESV

John the Revelator alludes to the Day of the Lord at least twice (Revelation 6:17; 16:14), so we know this isn't just some weird Pauline shout-out to the past.

The big one, though, comes in Paul's 2nd letter to the church at Thessalonica. Paul begins chapter two this way:

> *Now concerning the coming of our Lord Jesus Christ*
> *and our being gathered together to him,*
> *we ask you, brothers, not to be quickly*
> *shaken in mind or alarmed,*
> *either by a spirit or a spoken word,*

or a letter seeming to be from us,
to the effect that the day of the Lord has come.
2 Thessalonians 2:1-2 ESV

Paul is worried that folks are being convinced that they're living in a post-Day of the Lord world. He goes on to tell them what must first happen before said day:

Let no one deceive you in any way.
For that day will not come, unless
the rebellion comes first,
and the man of lawlessness is revealed,
the son of destruction, who opposes
and exalts himself
against every so-called god or object of worship,
so that he takes his seat in the temple of God,
proclaiming himself to be God.
2 Thessalonians 2:3-4 ESV

Whoa, nelly! This is an intense and odd passage! Whoever this man of lawlessness is, he sounds an awful lot like the dudes we hear about in Revelation. Could it be that this is another Biblical attestation of the *Left Behind* eschatology? Could it be that Kirk Cameron is an honest actor?

Whoever this bozo is, Paul says he'll claim God's throne. Now the question returns: when? When will all this crazy go down?

And you know what is restraining him now
so that he may be revealed in his time.

For the mystery of lawlessness is already at work.
Only he who now restrains it will do
so until he is out of the way.
And then the lawless one will be revealed,
whom the Lord Jesus will kill with
the breath of his mouth
and bring to nothing by the appearance of his coming.
2 Thessalonians 2:6-8 ESV

Paul's wording is intriguing: "the mystery of lawlessness". In Ephesians, Paul repeatedly refers to "the mystery of Christ" (Eph 3:4-6) and "the mystery of the Gospel" (Eph. 6:19). There seems to be some parallelism going on.

Chris's Interruption: Objection!

Just read one more verse, you ignoramus!

Dante's Rebuttal: Sustained

Fine, Chris, though it was unpleasant to hear you call me such an abominable word, I will give in to your contextual appeal.

The coming of the lawless one is
by the activity of Satan
with all power and false signs and wonders...
2 Thessalonians 2:9

You may point to this and say, "ah-ha! Look, the lawless one (who you are attempting to conclude is the Antichrist) can't be Satan! Satan is controlling him, so that can't be the same dude!"

To combat that line of reasoning, I need to go back to your main argument. You used John's letters to conclude that there are many antichrists, therefore there can't be one. As it turns out, when we look at the Day of the Lord, we can find multiple li'l Days before the Big One that Joel and Paul anticipate. Ezekiel 30:3 talks of the Day of the Lord falling on Egypt, and all of its wealth being taken away. It was not long after Ezekiel's writing that the Seleucid Dynasty came in and claimed Egypt for themselves. Similarly, Isaiah 34:8-9 warns Edom of the Lord's Day. Have you spoken to any Edomites lately? Turns out, a li'l Day of the Lord snuffed out those folks over two millennia ago. Despite these multiple Days of the Lord, Paul writes precisely about a singular event that must be preceded by several specific events before it can happen. This is, presumably, a tool that Biblical writers utilize: multiple appearances before the final realization. So, by the properties of osmosis, many antichrists don't preclude the existence of a singular antichrist.

Now, back to our regularly scheduled programming. It does at first seem odd that the term "antichrist" doesn't appear in Revelation, a book steeped in detailing the various degrees of God's retribution on those who've opposed him. Nor does the term appear in any of Paul's writings. From this, then, it appears that John's pet term for the disobedient one opposed to God is "Antichrist", while Paul's appears to be "'man of lawlessness".

Let's now come to Revelation. Notice the parallels between the events Paul says come before the Day of the Lord, and the actions of the dragon and beast:

> *And to it the dragon gave his power and*
> *his throne and great authority.*
> *One of its heads seemed to have a mortal wound,*
> *but its mortal wound was healed,*
> *and the whole earth marveled as*
> *they followed the beast.*
> *And they worshiped the dragon,*
> *for he had given his authority to the beast,*
> *and they worshiped the beast, saying,*
> *"Who is like the beast, and who can fight against it?"*
> Revelation 13:2-4 ESV

Here we have a figure that parodies Jesus. He is given power from the dragon (who is later named Satan in another Revelation passage), spreads lies, claims to be God, and has a resurrection-ish experience. This beast is a mockery of the Son of God, and Satan performs as a mockery of God the Father. But the passage doesn't end with just these two demonic figures...

> *Then I saw another beast rising out of the earth.*
> *It had two horns like a lamb and*
> *it spoke like a dragon...*
> *And it was allowed to give breath*
> *to the image of the beast,*

*so that the image of the beast might even speak
and might cause those who would not worship
the image of the beast to be slain.*
Revelation 13:11, 15 ESV

What's going on here? This new beast seems to be almost a carbon copy of the first. What's the point? Notice this phrase: "allowed to give breath". The Greek word for spirit and breath is the same: *pneuma* (think pneumonia--in the lungs). This "second beast" is providing a spirit/breath to the image of the beast. In other words, he's an unholy spirit.

Before the Day of the Lord, the one who opposes God will come to power. He'll use every trick in the book, and his newfound authority to mock God at every turn. He parodies the work of Christ on the cross. He parodies the trinity. Instead of God in three persons, the devil brings Satan in three persons; a cursed tri-beast.

You're right that John's letter proposes that anyone who denies Christ is an antichrist. But there is one, the Father of Lies, who is the ultimate antichrist. Paul and John have differing names for him, but his actions and aims are the same: aggregate power and mock God. This is the Antichrist. This is Satan.

Chris's Rebuttal: Satan is A Bad Parody
Do you remember the *Scary Movie* franchise?

The 2000s' comedy/horror movies were meant to parody other successful horror movies, particularly *Scream.* Surely, you remember them. Maybe you have fond memories of them, but I certainly don't. (I'm no film critic, but they were pretty terrible. Like hardly funny at all.) In case you're smitten with them, Rotten Tomatoes stands ready to remind you of its 42% rating and even includes this gem from one reviewer: "This movie will only frighten you with its crudeness."

Maybe terrible parody movies weren't your thing growing up, but you must have listened to Weird Al back in the day. Remember him? He's the dude who got famous playing the accordion and singing the corniest lyrics that could come to his mind in place of an original song's lyrics. Who doesn't love his *Star Wars*-themed *American Pie* cover, and where would satire be today without his juxtaposition of *Gangster's Paradise* as *Amish Paradise*? I get it; I loved me some Weird Al too, but go back and listen to one whole album and tell me you still would have this on any regular rotation. You are a liar. You wouldn't.

My point is parodies are often terrible. Sure, we may fondly remember that first trip to the movie theater to laugh at middle school humor in *Scary Movie* or the erratic dancing of a long-haired maniac mocking the Amish community, but eventually, these things grow tired. Parodies are based on novelty, and once they lose that power, there is little space left for them.

While I could argue with you that John and Paul's "Day of the Lord" is tied closely to the destruction and desecration of the Second Temple, I won't because I believe you are purposely tip-toeing around the problem at hand. Our disagreement seems to center fundamentally on one question: what is an antichrist?

For the record, I agree with you. Satan is clearly shown in the Scriptures as attempting to parody Jesus. The tri-beast in Revelation is almost all the proof one needs to see this. But this distinction is essential; Satan is *parodying* Christ.

The word antichrist isn't difficult to define; it implies that something or someone is the opposite of Christ. If Jesus is the greatest good, then calling something the antichrist would suggest it as the greatest evil; a foe perfectly designed to counter Christ. The yin to His yang.The belief that such a creature exists is Dualism in its simplest form, and it's wildly heretical.

Dualism is a belief system that masquerades itself within other belief systems. It's been around a long, long time and is simply the idea of separating something into two distinct, contrasting parts. It pops up pretty much anytime anyone talks about good and evil, and it's popped up for centuries in the Christian church.

Church fathers and heresy hunters spent a good amount of their time dealing with one dualistic belief called Gnosticism. The general idea of Gnostics was that everything physical was evil, while everything spiritual was good; two separate parts, the body and the spirit divided against each other. I fear that we have come to do this in our modern churches. We see Satan as one half of a coin with Jesus' face on the other end. It's why we use words to describe the "big bad" of Christianity as an antichrist. Paul seems to deal with the topic, or at least a precursor of it, constantly in passages like 1st Corinthians 15:1-58, Colossians 1:1-29, and 1st Timothy 6:20-21.

If Paul and the other church fathers were constantly railing against the tenets of dualism, then why would all that change in 2nd Thessalonians? My belief: it doesn't. Paul does not construct a big bad opposite to Christ. He shows us that Satan is a parody. In Paul and John's escheological remarks, Satan only appears to have any real power before being easily defeated by Christ. Satan's power is finite, and compared to the Messiah, it's laughable.

So then why does John say we can be antichrists? As I stated before, John shows that the actions we take can be antithetical to Christ. John isn't arguing that these people are the opposite of Christ, just that their actions and works are the opposite of His teaching. It takes the idea of Dualism that was likely present in the early churches he is writing to and shows it as a path not to be followed.

The long and short of it remains this; Satan is no more the antichrist than Weird Al is the antiCoolio.

Dante's Rebuttal: Perversion is the Key

"Satan doesn't create, he perverts" was one of the Christianese sayings I grew up with in the church. Frequently, this sentiment was followed by using the example of sex: sex is meant for good, but Satan has perverted the God-honoring practice in myriad ways. Since no one but God can create *ex nihilo*, the only tool that the enemy of God has is to contort, twist, and denigrate what God has made.

Your Weird Al example is prescient (your *Scary Movie* reference, on the other hand, isn't worth remembering -- I am a worse human for having watched those movies... God have mercy on my soul). Coolio's 1995 billboard topper, *Gangsta's Paradise,* was a phenomenon. It was also a raw, emotional work by the artist, who envisaged the song as a spiritual. What a cool idea: a spiritual for the hip-hop age. Then came *Amish Paradise.* The album's cover depicts Weird Al lifting a fedora off his head to reveal out-of-control cornrows, a culturally inappropriate appropriation that wouldn't fly a generation later. The image is particularly insensitive because Coolio iconically sported the cornrow look. When Coolio received a Grammy for *Gangsta's Paradise*, Weird Al was there, taking up space in the collective's imagination. Backstage that night, a reporter asked Coolio what he thought of *Amish Paradise*. Coolio responded:

> "I ain't with that...I think that my song was too serious...I really...don't appreciate him desecrating the song like that... his record company asked for my permission, and I said no. But they did it anyway..."

It's reminiscent of Antiochus IV going into the temple and desecrating it with a pig sacrifice, no?

But it's just a parody, right? No biggie...

Look at Coolio's career versus that of Weird Al. The latter has continued to remain in the collective zeitgeist while Coolio has never matched the success of *Gangsta's Paradise*. Weird Al slithered into Coolio's paradise and spoiled even the accomplishment of winning a Grammy.

Your reasoning seems to be based on the concept that the Antichrist can't be Satan because he's not God's equal. But maybe the old Sunday school true-ism actually has teeth: Satan can't create, he can only pervert. If Satan can't create, wouldn't it make sense that his biggest gambit would be finding a way to mock Jesus?

Chris's Rebuttal: Satan Cannot Rival Christ

You think you're pretty clever, don't you? But here's a twist for you; I agree with your premise. Satan can't create, he can only pervert, and that's because he isn't Christ's equal.

Turns out, the Coolio-Weird Al feud encapsulates my argument perfectly. As you said, Weird Al could have never made *Amish Paradise* a generation later. It's wildly inappropriate. Sure, Weird Al has had a more lucrative career than Coolio, but it's not because of *Amish Paradise*.

As of this writing, Weird Al's *Amish Paradise* has been viewed on Youtube 72 million times. Impressive for sure, but compare that to *Gangsta's Paradise*'s 609 million views, and it looks insignificant. Weird Al's song doesn't even have 15% what Coolio's does. Could it be that the funny at the time, but now inappropriate song has run its course in the collective zeitgeist? That's not to mention that Coolio won a grammy for his work, and Ol' Al didn't even get a nomination. Sure, Weird Al's career has been more successful since then. But Coolio stopped releasing new music in 2009 primarily because he didn't need to. *Gangsta's Paradise* topped the charts as a #1 single; something Weird Al still hasn't been able to accomplish in his four-decade career.

So can parody rival its original work? Weird Al's

case would suggest not. Your visceral reaction to the *Scary Movie* franchise proves this point even further.

So Satan's best option is to make fun of and mock Jesus? Sure, but only because he has little to no other options. Satan cannot equal God. He can twist God's creation to suit his desire in the same way you and I can too, but that doesn't make us gods. The ultimate promise of Scripture is God's renewal of all things, even the things the old devil tries to pervert. There is no Anti-Christ because there is no real rival to Christ. Therefore, Satan cannot be the Anti-Christ because he holds no power over the one who "makes all things new."

DEBATE IV

Is Satan the Nothing?

**Dante's Statement: Satan is the Villain
of *The Neverending Story***
The answer is philosophically straightforward.
Augustine solved it 1600 years ago.

> God created all things.
> All things God created are good.
> Therefore, evil is not a thing.

If God is love, then Satan must be love's opposite,
right? Generally, we call that anti-love, hate. I like
to call it evil. Satan is evil. You see where I'm going
with this… Satan is evil, and evil is not a thing.
That means that Satan can't be anything. He is the
absolute embodiment of nothing.

Next question: what is nothing?

Absence.

Darkness.

God's first words in Genesis is a curse on darkness.
Let there be light. Psalms 119:105 states, *Your word*

is a lamp to my feet, and a light to my path. Then John promptly tells us at the head of his Gospel that, *In the beginning was the word, and the word was with God, and the Word was God.* This Word is light, and this light is God. What is the purpose of the light? John tells us just two verses later, *The light shines in the darkness, and the darkness has not overcome it.* Wade into the waters of John's Gospel a little deeper, and eventually, you'll find Jesus saying, *I have come into the world as light, so that whoever believes in me may not remain in darkness.*

Paul, the great orator of divine theology, gives us our identity in Ephesians 5:8; *For at one time you were darkness, but now you are light in the Lord. Walk as children of light.* James, the brother of Jesus, explains how we too can exude the light: *Every good gift and every perfect gift is from above, coming down from the Father of lights with whom there is no variation or shadow due to change* (James 1:17). And lastly, to wrap this all nicely up in a bow, at the very end of the Bible, the very end of the very last book, when everything is finished, the story is told, everything, everything, EVERYTHING IS DONE... this will happen: *And the city has no need of sun or moon to shine on it, for the glory of God gives it light, and its lamp is the Lamb* (Rev. 21:23). It's all spelled out for you right there. Dark vs. Light, Good v. (the Nothingness of) Evil. It's just as John 1:5 states, *The light shines in the darkness, and the darkness has not overcome it.* Game. Set. Match.

Chris's Statement: Nothing Does Not Exist

So the story of Jesus is little more than that of *Star Wars*? Light vs. dark, good vs. evil, with no gray areas whatsoever. I suppose Dan Harmon was right when he said, "Every good story is just a retelling of the story of Jesus."

Can Satan really be nothing? If we are going to claim that, we need to understand better what nothing is. It should be an easy task as even three-year-olds can understand the concept of an empty container. But this is something that keeps scientists up at night. What nothing is has stumped the brightest minds among us. For a good reason too. The more you explore the subject, the stranger everything gets.

Now, let me make a huge disclaimer here. I am no scientist, and the topic which I'm going to dive into is very complicated. I would be a fool to attempt to explain the complete ins-and-outs of something like this. So, this will be a basic understanding of a subject I am not remotely qualified to elaborate on. Are you ready for a confusing statement?

Dante's Response: Objection

I am not ready.

Chris's Response: Overruled

Nothing isn't really *nothing*.

In the 1920s, scientists thought a complete vacuum could be created inside a box by removing all gases inside and cooling that box to absolute zero. They believed that when the box was observed, we would finally be able to view a space containing absolutely nothing. However, that's not what the scientists found. Instead, they saw that there were measurable fluctuations of energy inside the supposed empty vacuum. At first, this was believed to be a fluke, but the more scientists tested, the more they observed this spontaneous energy. They called this Zero Point Energy (ZPE) because they perceived energy in a situation devoid of all matter with zero energy value. All this was well and good, but it meant little unless this observed energy could affect the real world.

Enter Hendrick Casimir, who devised a simple device that could be inserted into a vacuum and harness the ZPE to draw two metal plates together. Big whoop, right? Casimir succeeded in proving to the scientific community that ZPE affected the real world. That means that we cannot discount the notion that something exists even when there appears to be nothing.

Many modern scientists have put forth theories about what ZPE means and its relation to the idea of nothing. Some have speculated that this energy is what produces the force of gravity. Others have concluded that ZPE is the minimum energy any area can have. We simply don't know enough about it to make a definitive statement other than the idea that where nothing is, *something* is present.

Let's step back into the field I'm a little more comfortable with: theology. You have made one fatal flaw in your reading of the Scripture. You have conflated God with light. A common descriptor of God is indeed the word light, and John certainly gives us this great light vs. dark scheme in his writings. But just because God emanates light within several Scriptural accounts does not make Him light. You have fallen into science's most deadly sin, assuming correlation equals causation.

How can I be so confident? I've got a big boy named King David on my side. Observe:

> *Where could I go to get away from your spirit?*
> *Where could I go to escape your presence?*
> *If I went up to heaven, you would be there.*
> *If I went down to the grave, you would be there too!*
> *If I could fly on the wings of dawn,*
> *stopping to rest only on the far side of the ocean—*
> *even there your hand would guide me;*
> *even there your strong hand would hold me tight!*
> *If I said, "The darkness will definitely hide me;*
> *the light will become night around me,"*
> *even then the darkness isn't too dark for you!*

> *Nighttime would shine bright as day,*
> *because darkness is the same as light to you!*
> Psalm 139:7-12 CEB

According to David, God exists in both the dark and the light. So why then would John give us the picture he does? I think John was using a metaphor even a child could understand; dark vs. light. When we watch *Star Wars* today, we don't believe that literal darkness is the presence of Darth Vader. If we did, that would completely recontextualize the planet of Dagoba. The same is true with God. Just because John uses darkness and light doesn't mean we should take it as literal darkness and literal light.

King David is describing God's omnipresence, which is a core tenet of who we know God is. Omnipresence means that God is always present; He is everywhere. We can conclude that God exists even in the darkness.

Science has discovered this Zero Point Energy exists even where there is nothing. This lines up surprisingly well with our understanding of God's omnipresence. If I were to hypothesize why ZPE exists, I would say that it's because God exists. If nothing can exist without there being something, I would postulate that it's because God is there. This is a confusing sentiment best summed up by Dan Smith when he wrote, "Where there is nothing there is God. God is everywhere."

Satan cannot be nothing simply because nothing does not exist.

DEBATE V

Is Satan Azazel?

Dante's Opening Statement: Satan is the Demon Known as Azazel

Let's start this one with Leviticus, shall we?

> *Then he shall take the two goats and*
> *set them before the Lord*
> *at the entrance of the tent of meeting.*
> *And Aaron shall cast lots over the two goats,*
> *one lot for the Lord and the other lot for Azazel.*
> Leviticus 16:7-8 ESV

Who is this Azazel? The rest of the Bible is mum on the word.

The goat for Azazel is not sacrificed to the Lord like the other, but rather:

> *...shall be presented alive before the Lord*
> *to make atonement over it,*
> *that it may be sent away*
> *into the wilderness to Azazel.*
> Leviticus 16:10 ESV

This passage is already weird enough, but then God goes and doubles down on the significance of this live-free-or-die-Azazel goat:

> *And Aaron shall lay both his hands*
> *on the head of the live goat,*
> *and confess over it all the iniquities*
> *of the people of Israel,*
> *and all their transgressions, all their sins.*
> *And he shall put them on the head of the goat*
> *and send it away into the wilderness*
> *by the hand of a man who is in readiness.*
> Leviticus 16:21 ESV

Catch that? *All their sins.*
Not one.
Not some.
All.

If this was the totality of what we knew about Azazel, well then you could chalk it up to some sort of weird pre-Jesus Biblical allusion.

Enter the Book of Enoch.

Enoch's book is a pseudepigraphal account pretending to be written by the Biblical Enoch, the dude that got drafted up to Team Heaven sans dying. The manuscript doesn't show up for thousands of years after Enoch's departure, so it's safe to say that it didn't come from our beloved Ascended E. Despite the dubious authorship, scholars think there's a good chance that parts of the Book of Enoch were exchanged orally for generations before being inked onto papyrus.

Enoch is a crazy book. It's sort of the Judaic version of the book of Revelation. Crazy stuff goes down in it. Perhaps the craziest of the crazy stuff is an extrapolation of Genesis 6 and the fall of some very naughty angels. In the Enochian account, a bunch of angels descend to earth to teach menfolk a bunch of lessons... and fornicate with some of the womenfolk. According to Enoch, Azazel was one of these angels. Azazel's stone-age classes must have been uber-popular. The dude apparently taught warfare, sword making, make-up application, body piercing, and witchcraft! That's a fabulous cross-section of subject matter!

The whammy comes in one verse: "The whole earth has been corrupted through the works that were taught by Azazel: to him ascribe all sin (Enoch 10:8)."

So, let's get this straight. Jesus calls Satan the "Father of lies" (John 8:44). Paul refers to unsaved folks as "sons of disobedience" (Ephesians 2:2). Ezekiel (28) and Isaiah (14) describe Satan as a "signet of perfection" and someone who has "fallen from heaven." I think it's safe to say that these Satanic descriptors don't sound like a human entity. It certainly sounds like Satan is (or was) an angel.

God himself tells his high priest in Leviticus to

ascribe all sin to Azazel. Enoch informs us that Azazel is an angel that taught mankind all sorts of insubordinate stuff.

While there are lots of evil angels with names in the book of Enoch, only one of them shows up in the actual Bible. And not only is Azazel present in the Bible, but God essentially orders a sacrifice to him!

Read Leviticus 16 again. There are two goats sacrificed as a sin offering. One goes to Yahweh. The other to Azazel. It's implicit right there in the text. Azazel is the yang to Yahweh's yin.

**Chris's Opening Statement: Satan
has Nothing to do with Azazel**
Oh, buddy, that's a pretty airtight case. I'm impressed, honestly. But, it seems your whole argument hinges on one crucial question; who is Azazel? However, to quote Jesus Himself:

> *You're asking the wrong questions.*
> John 9:4a MSG

I'm getting ahead of myself. Let's deal with the low-hanging fruit first: 1st Enoch.

To your credit, you mentioned the book is a bit on the wild side. But come on, man, you've left out the best part: COSMIC SPACE TREES. That's right. Cosmic. Space. Trees. A whole chapter dedicated just to them. That's just the tip of the iceberg for Enoch too. Calling the book crazy is an understatement. It makes Revelation look tame.

To your discredit, you've seriously downplayed the significant issues with the book's trustworthiness. For starters, even the most lenient scholars only date the book to 300 BCE. Even IF 1st Enoch were passed down orally for several generations before then, you'd be hard-pressed to say it was in circulation before the beginning of Second Temple Judaism. Sure, Leviticus is typically dated as a finished work around 535 BCE, BUT we have far more certainty the Torah was passed orally for hundreds of years before the start of Second Temple Judaism.

Then there's the issue of the entire book: we don't have it. Well, we do kind of, but it's complicated. We have eleven scraps translated from Aramaic and only three tiny fragments of Hebrew, which should be the original language of the book if it was passed down orally by the Jews. Instead, the bulk of the book we have comes from the language Ge'ez of the Ethiopian people. Now, I don't want beef with the Ethiopian church here. They have a wide and deep faith tradition that spans thousands of years. The problem is that we know nothing about how the Ethiopian copy came into existence. Scholars have speculated on how the book could have wound up there, but due to Ethiopia's isolation from the west for nearly a millennium, the speculation remains just that. There is some speculation in dating and even translating all ancient documents, however, the amount of guesstimation with 1st Enoch is on a whole other level.

Though Leviticus only dates 500 years earlier than 1st Enoch, we have fragments of the Priestly Code sections from the 7th and 9th centuries. 1st Enoch didn't come onto the scene until late first-century BCE; literally hundreds of years later. Keep in mind Enoch allegedly lived some 6,000 years before this, and that's being extremely generous with the Biblical timeline. If the Hebrews passed it down orally, that's an abnormally long game of telephone.

The absolute worst part of it all? 1st Enoch is like the Pumpkin Spice Latte of ancient texts. Every Christian who wants to dabble in other ancient texts ALWAYS reads it first and ALWAYS thinks they have stumbled onto something game-changing. In reality, they've only found out about some terrible tasting brown water that is way overhyped.

But enough about 1st Enoch and its sketchy origins. I mentioned that I believe you are asking the wrong question. You are asking a question that presumes a specific answer, but it's still the wrong question. As such, you've arrived at the wrong answer. You are asking "*Who* is Azazel?" when you really should be asking "*Where* is Azazel?"

It's an easy mistake to make. The

pseudepigraphical books all suppose the same thing: Azazel is an entity. However, Leviticus doesn't tell us Azazel is a person. Azazel is a name, but not the name of a being. It's the name of a place.

Let's back up.

As you pointed out, Leviticus 16 describes a ceremony. The Israelites are to take two goats and cast lots over them. One lot will fall to Yahweh. That goat is to be killed and offered to Him. From what we know of the Israelite people, this makes a lot of sense. As I noted previously, the animals killed in their sacrifices acted as stand-ins for the peoples' own lives, hence why the animal has to die. So, killing the goat and giving it as a burnt offering makes sense.

But now think about the second goat. Aaron is supposed to lay his hands on the goat's head and confess all the sins of the entire nation. Knowing Israel, that's going to take a hot minute. The weird bit is that he is supposed to send it into the wilderness after confessing all the nation's sins. That's right, Aaron is supposed to free that poor goat to live the rest of its life. It's like releasing a spider back into the wild instead of power slamming your boot on it.

If this ritual is a sacrifice to some deity that is the "yin to Yahweh's yang", it doesn't make any sense because that's not a *sacrifice*.

Animal sacrifices are supposed to substitute for the lives of Israelites, but that's not what's going on here. Instead, this animal is allowed to live, to escape with its life! One might even call it an escaped goat. Wait. Escaped-goat? Scapegoat? Oh! It's not a sacrifice at all; it's meant to act as a scapegoat for the Israelites. That's why it's released into the wilderness and not killed.

But where does Azazel fit into this? The rabbis during the Second Temple period of Judaism (who were contemporaries at the same time the book of 1st Enoch was written) had a pretty shocking answer to this. They traced the word back to its original Hebrew roots; *Azaz*, which meant "rugged," and *el*, which meant "strong or mighty." They concluded that "Azazel" wasn't a deity but a mountain range within the wilderness. For this reason, a myriad of different Biblical translations translate the word instead of leaving the Hebrew name. The CSB translates as "the uninhabitable place". The NLT calls it the "wilderness of Azazel", obviously a place. The overwhelming majority, NIV, BSB, NASB, ISV, heck even the freakin' King James Version (KJV), replaces the word with the term "scapegoat". Look where we've ended up; I'm agreeing with the KJV! Who am I!?!?

It should be pretty clear by now that the scapegoat is no "sacrifice". Instead, the live goat represents Yahweh's forgiveness of the nation's sins. Azazel isn't some mega-demon-daddy. That belief is some fan-fiction nonsense with no Biblical support. Azazel never shows up as Satan or is ever even correlated to Satan in the Biblical account. It's pretty safe to say there is no "yin to Yahweh's yang".

Dante's Recap: Chris's Argument Distilled Down

You said you were impressed "honestly", but I don't feel like you were actually impressed.

Sigh.

So as to not let your various points fall asunder, let me try to list your arguments:

-1st Enoch is too weird to count toward anything.

-The dating and reliability of 1st Enoch is suspect.

-The word Azazel means "uninhabited place" and is therefore referring to a location rather than an entity.

-The sacrifice was not a sacrifice, but a 'scapegoat'.

Does that about cover it?

Chris's Recap: I'll Do My Own Summarizing, Thank You Very Much

Close, but I'd better sum it up like this:

-1st Enoch lacks the narrative structures consistent with the narrative put forward by the

Scriptures up to its "alleged" date.

    -1st Enoch's dating and reliability aren't suspect; they're impossible.

    -Yeah, no, that pretty much sums up #3.

    -The goat wasn't killed in a sacrificial manner and thus can't be called a proper sacrifice by Israelite standards.

Now that we've cleared that up, you may continue with your case.

Dante's Rebuttal: Your Arguments Aren't Worth the Spit They Took to Say

Alright, let's plow through these one-by-one.

You've decided to throw the book of Enoch, and for some reason, the Ethiopian church, under the bus (or over the cliff, as we'll soon see)--

Chris's Interruption: Objection!

Objection! I clearly stated I wanted no beef with the Ethiopian church.

Dante's Response: Fine, I'll Leave the Ethiopians Out of the Conversation

Just hear me out, Jerkface.

Chris's Interruption: Fair Enough.

You may continue, but counsel be warned, you are on thin ice!

Dante's Rebuttal Continued: Your Arguments Aren't Worth the Spit They Took to Say

Your point about the dating of Enoch is not without merit. The date is late, granted. It's also missing pieces. Doubly granted. But you failed to mention that, according to most scholars, 1st Enoch should really be 1st, 2nd, 3rd, 4th and 5th Enoch. This makes, by the way, the other books currently entitled 2nd and 3rd Enoch actually 6th and 7th Enoch. That's more Enochs than there are Rocky movies! Making matters worse, we've found different fragments of the book in Greek, Latin, Hebrew, and Aramaic, adding further muddiness to the question of the book's origins.

The most widely copied section, and almost assuredly the oldest and most complete section, however, is the story of the fallen angels that parallels (or expands) upon Genesis 6. For our sakes, I think the dating of the book is mostly irrelevant. Enoch holds a unique place in the Christian tradition for two reasons: (1) it serves as an early entrant in the apocalyptic literature genre, and (2) it's referenced in both Jude and 2nd Peter.

Here's the Jude example:

> *It was also about these that Enoch,*
> *the seventh from Adam, prophesied, saying,*
> *"Behold, the Lord comes with ten*

thousands of his holy ones,
to execute judgment on all and to
convict all the ungodly
of all their deeds of ungodliness
that they have committed
in such an ungodly way, and of all the harsh things
that ungodly sinners have spoken against him."
Jude 14-15 ESV

And here's Enoch 1:9:

> "And behold! He cometh with ten thousands of His holy ones to execute judgement upon all, and to destroy all the ungodly: And to convict all flesh of all the works of their ungodliness which they have ungodly committed, and of all the hard things which ungodly sinners have spoken against Him."

Jude's not merely quoting Enoch. According to Pastor David C. Curtis of Berean Bible Church, Jude "also follows the content patterns of 1 Enoch along with allusions and echoes of its phrases and language throughout his Epistle." Ditto goes for Enochian allusions in 2nd Peter.

Enoch may not be canon, but the disciples of Jesus paid close attention to it. The book certainly warrants more contemplation and grace from us than mere "SPACE TREES!" defamations.

Speaking of "SPACE TREES!", Enoch is clearly written as an apocalyptic tome. This particular literary genre that began to blossom in the Ancient Near East during the Hellenistic era (and continued on through Roman rule) is a tough nut for us modern readers to crack. If apocalyptic literature was easy to decipher, we'd all be much better friends with the book of Revelation. What we do know is that apocalyptic literature often uses fantastical language to speak to current issues facing the writer's generation. And what's so wrong with SPACE TREES anyway?! They sound awesome!

Moving right along...

I'll need some help from my Jewish friends over at jewishvirtuallibrary.org to go over this "Azazel is a place" business.

Leviticus doesn't give us a whole lot of insight into how the Azazel sacrifice (or scapegoating, as you put it) went down. To understand the logistics of the ritual, we are reliant upon the Mishnah. The Mishnah was a series of commentaries written by Jewish priests that essentially gave exegesis on the Hebrew Bible verse by verse. Much of this was composed during the 2nd Temple period. That places it, most likely: post Old Testament, pre-New Testament. Thankfully, the Mishnah goes into great detail as to how the Azazel ritual is supposed to go down.

As the priests explain, a crimson thread is wrapped around the Azazel goat, the high priest imputes the sins of the people onto said goat via thumbs to the forehead, and then a priest walks the goat to a high cliff. According to jewishvirtuallibrary.org, at this cliff, the priest "pushed the goat over it backward and it hardly reached the halfway mark in its descent before it was completely dismembered."

The goat may be escaping, but only into the jaws of death. The scapegoat carries the sins of the people into death.

Now, let's talk about that name again: *Azazel*. You played fast and loose with me, defining the last two letters of the word as "strong or mighty". Are you playing fair, dear pastor?

El is an ancient word. It is used as a name for God multiple times in the Hebrew Bible. Most often, *El* is connected to other words to make God stand out: *El Shaddai* (God of glory), *El Elyon* (God most high), *El Gibbor* (God of strength), *El Roi* (God the shepherd), and several others. More frequently than any of those names, *El* is used as a plural word for God in the form of "Elohim", which is the title given to God hundreds of times in our Biblical text. That's not all: think on the nation of Israel. Isra-EL is originally the name bestowed upon Jacob, the fella who fought with God. The name literally translates as "wrestled with God". Then, of course, we have Dani-EL (God's judgment), Micha-EL (who is like God), and Gabri-EL (strength of God). Last but not least, come Christmastime, we herald in the arrival of the baby born in Bethlehem, prophesied as being Immanu-EL (God with us).

When we look outside of the Hebrew tradition, we continue to see the word *El* used in rarified air. The Canaanites, the nearby folk that the Israelites are always coming toe-to-toe with, worshipped a pantheon of gods. Wanna take a guess at who their supreme god was? Their god above all the other gods was named… wait for it…

EL.

So, it is not only understandable to see Azaz-EL and think that the name must have some deified significance; it's the most rational explanation.

One last point needs to be made. Our text for this Azazel character is found in Leviticus 16. Right next door, in the very next chapter, we get this odd verse:

> *So they shall no more sacrifice*
> *their sacrifices to goat demons,*
> *after whom they whore.*
> *This shall be a statute forever for them*
> *throughout their generations.*
> Leviticus 17:7 ESV

Forgive me, but I must quote Ellicot's Commentary here at some length, for he melds together several of our pressing concerns:

The word here translated "devils," literally denotes hairy or shaggy goats, and then goat-like deities, or demons. The Egyptians, and other nations of antiquity, worshipped goats as gods. Not only was there a celebrated temple in Thmuis, the capital of the Mendesian Nomos in Lower Egypt, dedicated to the goat-image Pan, whom they called Mendes, and worshipped as the oracle, and as the fertilising principle in nature, but they erected statues of him everywhere. Hence the Pan, Silenus, satyrs, fauns, and the woodland gods among the Greeks and Romans; and hence, too, the goat-like form of the devil, with a tail, horns, and cloven feet, which obtain in medieval Christianity, and which may still be seen in some European cities. The terror which the devil, appearing in this Pan-like form, created among those who were thought to have seen him, has given rise to our expression panic. This is the form of idolatrous worship which the Jews brought with them from Egypt, and to which reference is continually made.

Here's what I'm advocating for: don't de-godify the Ancient Near East.

Yahweh concerns himself with other entities multiple times in the Old Testament. In many cases, the deities are not merely swiped away as mindless idols of the people's imagination. No, the gods have teeth. This makes us, stout monotheists, very uneasy. But maybe God is saying something important here with Azazel/Pan/Satan. He's mocking them. "Yeah, demon, I'll make sure the people give you something... but instead of the first fruits, the unspotted calf, the best of the best, you'll get the sins of the people and a goat whose every bone has been broken."

[Wondering what role demons play as opposed to Satan, check out Dante's analysis of Satan's worker bees in Addendum: Demons.]

Chris's Rebuttal: Quoting a Source Doesn't Make it Inspired

Those are fair points. I will make one concession and two counter-points. Concession: Azazel is likely referring to both a place and some Near East deity in Leviticus.

Counter-points:
1. Just because Jude and 2nd Peter quote scraps of 1st Enoch does not make it inspired.
2. Without Enoch, it becomes pretty messy to connect Satan directly to Azazel.

"Don't give a child a fish; show him how to fish." Good advice, right? Pretty similar to the modern phrase, "give a man a fish, and you feed him for a day, teach a man to fish, and you feed him for a lifetime." I wouldn't call you a communist for quoting this old phrase.

Then again, I might not be too far off.

"Don't give a child a fish, show him how to fish" is from *Mao's Little Red Book*, a widely hailed communist writing. Simply quoting something doesn't mean you endorse it 100%. But that's a silly example; let me give you a more practical one.

In his Epistle to Titus, Paul is complaining to Titus about some false teachers that have infected their church. These teachers were from the island of Crete, leading Paul to write:

> *Someone who is one of their own prophets*
> *said, 'People from Crete are always liars,*
> *wild animals, and lazy gluttons.*
> Titus 1:12 CEB

WOAH! Paul, calm down! Aside from the xenophobic stuff, it's important to note that Paul seems to be directly quoting *The Hymn to Zeus* by the Greek poet Callimachus, who may be quoting an earlier work by the poet Epimenides. I think for obvious reasons, you will not call *The Hymn of Zeus* inspired. I also think you'd be hard-pressed to say there is theological knowledge of God and His creation that we should pull out of it. Yet, Paul quotes it within an inspired work.

I can hear you winding up, "But Paul isn't teaching us anything about God from that verse!"

Okay, sure, but Paul does it again!

> *In God we live, move, and exist.*
> *As some of your own poets have said*
> *"We are his offspring"*
> Acts 17:28 CEB

This time Paul is quoting Aratus, a Cilician poet, and his work *Phaenomena 5*. Paul isn't quoting these Greek authors to tell us their work is inspired, just as Jude's quote doesn't claim the same thing.

What's more, Jude does it again too. At the very start of his short letter (which is just ripping off a bunch of authors, so can we even attribute the thing to him?), he recounts a story of Michael the Archangel and his refusal to rebuke Satan. This story is lifted from the pages of *The Assumption of Moses*, a 1st century BCE pseudepigraphal work supposed to be Moses revealing hidden secrets to Joshua. What do ya know? It's also an apocalyptic text!

Look, Second Temple Judaism is filled with pseudepigraphal, apocalyptic works. However, there are very valid reasons why we don't attribute inspiration to them, even if inspired sources quote from them. From them, we can draw any number of points about Satan that we want to, but it's all wild speculation at the end of the day.

I do not doubt the Jews believed they were sending

a scapegoat to an ancient deity. But to think they were sacrificing to Satan himself is a stretch that is not supported in Biblical texts. Could you imagine the Jews referring to the devil as "El" anything?

Dante's Conclusion: Every Bone Broken

It was important that not a bone in Christ's body was broken. That's why the Centurion had to stick him with the spear between the ribs instead of breaking his legs as was tradition. Jesus, the sacrificial lamb of God, dies with bones intact. Might it be more than coincidence that this scapegoat, who bears all the sins of the Israelites, has every bone in his body smashed as he falls over a cliff?

Perhaps God mocks.

DEBATE VI,VI,VI

Is Satan Mammon?

**Dante's Opening Statement: Satan
is the Love of Money**
I spent two years of my life teaching GED classes in a state prison. I had a student that had a massive forehead tattoo. What's the sentiment that he decided to engrave on his face for the rest of his life? Six. Six. Six.

Let's talk about this 666 business. We all go to bed holding firm to our precious little 666 verse from Revelation. Every schoolboy and schoollass is trained in the art of Revelation 666 recitation. I'm pretty sure if you fold up a twenty-dollar bill just right six ways sideways, you can find the whole verse splayed out in front of you like Sharon Stone in *Basic Instinct*.

Yes. Let's all recite it from memory now, class. Ready. Begin.

*This calls for wisdom:
let the one who has understanding*

> *calculate the number of the beast,*
> *for it is the number of a man,*
> *and his number is 666.*
> Revelation 13:8 ESV

This calls for wisdom. Yes, my little blueberries. Wisdom indeed… for while my fun numerologists contend that 666 is the Hebrew numberification of Emperor Nero taking a bath in a pool of first century Christian bone marrow, there's a much simpler and frickin' wiser place to look. How about this concept, my rump rutabagas: find wisdom in other places in the Bible!

As it turns out, Revelation isn't the only place 666 pokes its armored head out.

A cursory look at 2 Chronicles 9:13 (or its parallel in 1 Kings 10:14) looks innocuous; nothing more than a mere coincidence.

> *Now the weight of gold that came to Solomon*
> *in one year was 666 talents of gold…*
> 2 Chronicles 9:13 ESV

No biggie, right? Wrong-o, buck-o. Big biggie. Paul thinks so. Check it:

> *For the love of money is a root of all kinds of evils.*
> 1 Timothy 6:10 ESV

Paul not enough for you? Here's Jesus:

> *No one can serve two masters,*

for either he will hate the one and love the other,
or he will be devoted to the one and despise the other.
You cannot serve God and money.
Matthew 6:24 ESV

The word for money there is the Greek word *mammon*. Jesus continually speaks about how difficult it is for the rich to enter the kingdom of heaven. When the rich young ruler comes to Jesus inquiring about the cost of eternal life, Jesus replies simply that he must sell everything. Christ tells a dark tale about a rich man suffering in a hell-like place after death. It's a lot. Jesus blessed the poor and indigent while repeatedly warning the upper crust. Why?

Jesus' brother James even goes a step farther in his letter:

Come now, you rich,
weep and howl
for the miseries that are coming upon you.
James 5:1 ESV

I run too fast. Circle back to the 666 reference in 2 Chronicles: the wealth of Solomon. The context surrounding the number drop is a little confusing. Following the list of Solomon's riches is... his death. He was so rich... he had all this good stuff: gold and silver and spices and women and buildings and excess food... and he died.

Did his riches save him from death? By no means.

More insightful than what follows Solomon's 666 is the context that accompanies it. Enter: the Queen of Sheba. This cat waltzes into Solomon's life from an exotic, international locale, only to fall head over heels for our boy Shlomo. The story (in 2 Chronicles 9:4) reads like the first page of a steamy romance. Nobody knows for sure where this "Sheba" was exactly. Some see Sheba as being the same as Saba, a kingdom in present-day Yemen. Others vouch for Ethiopia. If either location proves true, then this queen was almost assuredly dark-skinned. That detail may link the female character in Song of Solomon to Queen Sheba herself:

> *I am black and beautiful,*
> *O daughters of Jerusalem,*
> *like the tents of Kedar,*
> *like the curtains of Solomon.*
> *Do not gaze at me because I am dark,*
> *because the sun has gazed on me.*
> Song of Solomon 1:5-6 NRSV

If the connection is real (if the Queen of Sheba = Solomon's lover), then what we got here, folks, is a love affair for the centuries.

Let's assume that the Queen of Sheba came from Ethiopia. This would help explain how the Ethiopian eunuch that shows up in the book of Acts has his claws on a copy of Isaiah. Fascinatingly, there is indeed an ancient strand of Ethiopian Jews, known as Beta Israel.

Remember when you shat on the Ethiopian church, Chris?

These Beta Israel folks have a long and deep cultural heritage, as do the Ethiopian Orthodox Christians. The Ethiopian Christians claim their faith lineage from the apostle Philip and the Ethiopian dude Phil led to conversion. And dig this: Ethiopia is the only African country that can claim to have never been a colony of another nation (well, maybe Liberia also qualifies, but their nationalism only dates back to the mid-19th century). The point here is two-fold:

1) Ethiopians have deep Judeo-Christian roots.
2) They have a unique African history.

So, what exactly is the origin story for these Ethiopian Jews? Some think that the rogue tribe of Dan migrated there way back when. But another theory claims that Solomon took the Queen of Sheba into his bed-chamber.

> *Your stature is like a palm tree,*
> *and your breasts are like its clusters.*
> *I say I will climb the palm tree*
> *and lay hold of its fruit.*
> Song of Solomon, 7:7-8 ESV

As the theory goes…
The Queen had a son on her way back to Sheba. That son became king. He, obviously, was Jewish. According to the *Kebra Nagast*, a compendium of Ethiopian tales, when this Ethiopian/Jewish dude

(name: Menelik) becomes a man, he decides to take an international walkabout to meet his Papa for the first time. He travels to Jerusalem where Solomon is overjoyed to meet him. Sol is so overjoyed, in fact, that he tries to convince Menelik to succeed him as king of Israel. Mene politely says no. He has to return to Ethiopia. Sheba ain't gonna rule itself. Gotta lock down that empire and keep it clean from colonizers. The young man returns back home. Solomon, as a weird sort of peace offering, sends a bundle of first-born elder sons with Menelik. These sons of Israel are to live as Sheba-ites for the rest of their lives. That has to be a tough pill to swallow for the young men. Understandably, these "first sons" are pretty bent out of shape by this whole sudden situation. So, they decide to do what many-a-forsaken folk does: they steal stuff. But not just any old stuff. They steal the Ark.

Yep. The Ark of the Covenant was taken to Ethiopia. At least, so goes the story. And lest you think this is just a folktale to make Ethiopians feel nationalistic, take a look at the largest denomination in Ethiopia: the Ethiopian Orthodox Tewahedo Church. This church claims not only that the Queen of Sheba/Ark story is true; they claim they still have the Ark to this day. That's right, Chris! Turns out the Nazis didn't steal it from Indiana Jones after all! It's been in Ethiopia for 2,500 years this whole friggin' time!

The Church of Our Lady Mary of Zion says they got it. They built a holy of holies to put it in, but uh... you can't see it. Only the "guardian monk" gets to take a look-see at it. And that dude serves time like a pope. Once a "guardian monk" is chosen, he serves the Ark for life.

While it's understandable that this Ark business raises some skeptical eyebrows, riddle me this, Batman: what happened to the Ark? In the Biblical narrative, after Solomon, it seemingly falls off the face of the Earth. It's nowhere to be found. Gonzo.

Why?

Why the Queen of Sheba? Why the missing Ark? Why this curse on rich people? Why 666? Why, why, why?

Because Satan is Mammon.
Solomon has all the wisdom in the world. And yet, because of Solomon's sons, Israel breaks into two, all the wealth eventually evaporates, and the Ark disappears.

> *Your riches have rotted and your*
> *garments are moth-eaten.*
> *Your gold and silver have corroded,*
> *and their corrosion will be evidence against you*
> *and will eat your flesh like fire.*
> *You have laid up treasure in the last days.*
> James 5:2-3 ESV

In the middle ages, Mammon was iconographized

as a demon of Greed. Milton in *Paradise Lost* lists Mammon in the pantheon of hell. Mammon = Money = Greed. And Greed was there in the beginning. Greed is what tempted Eve. Her life wasn't good enough. She had to become like a god. That was the pull that led this world to destruction. Jesus said that you can't serve two masters. You either serve God... or you serve Mammon. Interesting that he didn't say "Beelzebub" or "Lucifer" or "Demons". He said. Mammon. You either serve God. Or you serve Mammon.

Mammon led the Ark out of Israel. He perverted Solomon. And his is the mark of the beast. What more evidence do you need?

Chris's Opening Statement: Let's Slow Down For A Second Mr. Hare

Money is the root of all evil. That's it, case closed. Paul even says so, *right?*

As you said, Dante, you're a fast runner. Allow me to be the tortoise to your hare. Let's slow it down for a second, starting with Paul. In 1st Timothy, Paul writes to his protégé, giving him loads of advice as any good mentor would. Timothy, a young pastor at the church in Ephesus, is having a rough go of it with his congregation. Given what we already know about the church in Ephesus, we shouldn't be shocked.

Five years earlier, Paul pens the letter of Ephesians

to the very people Timothy is struggling with. Paul always addresses issues he witnessed firsthand in the congregations he visited. One of those issues for the Ephesians is *greed*.

> *So I'm telling you this, and I insist on it in the Lord:*
> *you shouldn't live your life like the Gentiles anymore.*
> *They base their lives on pointless thinking,*
> *and they are in the dark in their reasoning.*
> *They are disconnected from God's life*
> *because of their ignorance and their closed hearts.*
> *They are people who lack all sense of right and wrong,*
> *and who have turned themselves over*
> *to doing whatever feels good*
> *and to practicing every sort of*
> *corruption along with greed.*
> Ephesians 4:17-19 CEB

Okay, so the Ephesian church loves it some money. Big whoop, right? That is until we look a little closer at Paul's counsel to Timothy.

> *Actually, godliness is a great source of profit*
> *when it is combined with being happy*
> *with what you already have.*
> *We didn't bring anything into the world and*
> *so we can't take anything out of it:*
> *we'll be happy with food and clothing.*
> *But people who are trying to get*
> *rich fall into temptation.*
> *They are trapped by many stupid*
> *and harmful passions*

that plunge people into ruin and destruction.
The love of money is the root of all kinds of evil.
Some have wandered away from the faith
and have impaled themselves
with a lot of pain because they
made money their goal.
1st Timothy 6:6-10 CEB

No devil there. What's more, Paul seems to place the blame on the *people* for causing their grief. Not the big red baddie. If that isn't enough to convince you, the final nail in the coffin is the Greek word Paul uses for money here. It stands to reason that if money lured away the Ephesians, Paul would have personified it. But the word he uses isn't a personification for money, instead, it's the Greek word *philarguria*. This isn't even a word for just money, but instead is a Greek word that translates to "the love of money." It's an action, not a person: no Mammon, no Satan.

What about Revelation and Solomon, though? We have an example of a "demonic" symbol in the New Testament correlating to a monetary sum in the Old Testament. That's a rare kind of continuity we don't always see between the Scriptures! But as a good ole' boy from my congregation is fond of saying, "It sure seems like you're fishing in the wrong pond. You've caught yourself a red-herring!"

Even though John tells us explicitly in Revelation

to *calculate* the number of the Beast, and that number adds up to a cryptograph of the name Nero Caesar, I'll humor you. Let's say that John does intend for 666 to be the name of Satan. Does Solomon's acquisition of 666 talents clearly tell us that the devil is in his finances? Well, I suppose that depends on *if* Solomon lost the Ark to the Ethiopians.

In full disclosure, we really should note that the Ethiopians aren't the only people to claim to have found the Ark. Nope, I'm not talking about Nazis either, though I suppose Speilberg should be included on this list. In 1982, an amateur explorer named Ron Wyatt claimed to have found the Ark in a cave under the city of Jerusalem. Much like our Ethiopian counterparts, he refused to show it to anyone. In a sense, he was appointing himself the sole guardian of the Ark.

The Ethiopians' claim is rooted in thousands of years of heritage and history. Indeed, that carries more weight than Indiana Wyatt's claim. *The Kebra Negast* is a historical document dating from the 14th century CE, allegedly recounting an untold story from the 10th century BCE. That's well over two thousand years removed from each other! Even by Biblical dating standards, that's insane.

But *The Kebra* isn't the first known reference of this tale. See, we have a slightly earlier source for this claim in the 12th century by Abu al-Makarim. Abu is a Coptic Orthodox priest who wrote a work called *History of Churches and Monasteries* in which he recounted a similar story of Ethiopians with Solomon-like features carrying off the Ark. How an Egyptian priest two thousand years in the future gets this information is unclear. To make matters worse, some scholars have speculated that Abu meant to say Europeans, not Ethiopians. Given all the evidence, it seems shaky at best that the Queen of Sheba, a nation we have no idea where it is or what it refers to, is the Queen of Ethiopia.

Alas! There is still one last group of people who claim to have special knowledge of where the Ark is: the Jewish people themselves. In the second century BCE, the deuterocanonical work 2nd Maccabees claims that the prophet Jeremiah hid the Ark in Mount Nebo sometime around the 7th century BCE (2nd Maccabees 2). That's 300 years after Solomon's Sheba encounter for those keeping track at home.

Is this work reliable? Well, it's written 500 years removed from Jeremiah's life, but still four times closer than Abu's tale of the Ethiopians. As early as 397 at the council of Carthage, the Maccabees were affirmed as canon. On top of all that, we know that some Jews believed this myth in Jesus' time.

In John 1, the Pharisees ask John the Baptist about

his true identity, offering various suggestions. One specific suggestion is "the prophet." We know the Pharisees aren't talking about Elijah because they ask about Elijah beforehand. Instead, the implication is that John is Jeremiah. They believed 2nd Maccabees claim that Jeremiah would come again and reveal the location of the Ark. The leading sect of the Jews thought that Jeremiah hid the Ark. Old Sheba couldn't possibly have taken it. Though the Ark has never been found at Nebo, it seems a steadier ground to stand on than the Ethiopian claim.

So, if Solomon didn't lose the Ark to the Ethiopians, does his acceptance of 666 talents mean anything? In short, no. Neither 1st Kings nor 2nd Chronicles add any negative connotations to the money, and the Queen's gifts are received as a celebration of Solomon's wisdom. The wisdom he received straight from God, no less. No Mammon here either.

Finally, we come to the most challenging of your claims. Jesus straight-up tells us Mammon is Satan.

It would vibe with Jesus' whole dunking on the rich deal. Time and time again, Jesus does condemn the rich and encourage the poor. I have no argument against that. Even the church fathers have your back here: Gregory of Nyssa names Mammon as the being Beelzebub, Jerome closely ties the name Mammon to greed, and golden voice John Chrysostom calls Mammon a greedy demon.

Ultimately, our debate centers around that one Greek word Jesus throws out in Matthew 6:24: *mammon.* Is Jesus naming the devil for us? It's hard to be entirely sure. Due to ancient Greek's annoying omission of capitalization and punctuation, it's still not possible for us to know.

It sure seems like Matthew doesn't use mammon as a proper name. Most modern translators translate the word to "money". This would be a surprising way for them to indicate that Matthew is naming someone. Plus, there is plenty of precedent in other ancient Greek writings that also use mammon when referring to currency. Nearly all trustworthy lexicons identify this word as a *thing*, not a *person*.

There are some rumors and myths that say Mammon could also refer to a Syrian god of money. But we have not found any documents, inscriptions, or actual references to this god in Syrian culture. The personification of mammon doesn't appear to be a thing before the 4th century.

Maybe Jesus didn't personify mammon because he didn't have sympathy for the devil. Poor Satan can't get no satisfaction. Jesus was a-rollin' stone. Okay, sorry, that was just too far.

Even if Jesus didn't want to give the devil his

due here, why not continue to name Mammon as Satan? Why not mention money in John 8? Why not spell it out for us? Because money is not the root of all evil. Instead, to paraphrase Paul, the love of money leads to evil.

Dante's Rebuttal: But there's Another Biblical Instance Too!

Ha! If I'm a hare, well sir, you forgot that this hare, much like Vin Diesel, always carries an extra tank of NOS with him! That's right, my pedantic little friend, I held back from you. There's another 666 Bible reference. WELCOME TO THE GUN SHOW!

> *The sons of Adonikam, 666.*
> Ezra 2:13 ESV

That's it. That's the whole verse. Need more context? Fine, you slow-ass turtle.

> *The sons of Azgad, 1,222.*
> *The sons of Adonikam, 666.*
> *The sons of Bigvai, 2,056.*
> Ezra 2:12-14 ESV

Take that limp biscuit and fry it up! Boom!

Chris's Rebuttal: Ezra 2 Means Literally Nothing

To be fair, I will concede that this is another occurrence of the number 666 in Scripture... BUT that hardly means anything at all.

In Ezra 2, we get this extensive list of Jews who get

to come back home after being exiled. It's about as fun as reading any of the long lists of genealogies the Bible likes to throw at us from time to time. I can understand how you may be looking for any way to stay awake while reading this passage. Upon seeing that infamous number, you spring from your chair shouting, "There he is! That tricky devil! I knew I'd find him!"

We Bible nerds have a terrible habit of thinking every correlation must equal some causation. Who are these sons of Adonikam? Who the heck is Adonikam? Unsurprisingly, they're nobodies. *Hitchcock's Bible Names Dictionary* tells us this name in Hebrew means "The Lord is raised". What should we make of that? Ancient Jews just really liked to give their children titles that mean things.

We don't get anything else about the sons of Adonikam or the man himself, other than in Ezra 8, they are numbered as coming in last. We only see them pop up one more time in the Biblical narrative in Nehemiah 7. What wisdom does old Nehemiah have to tell us about this family?

Of Adonikam 667
Nehemiah 7:18 CEB

Ooooooo so close, but no cigar, my man. Nehemiah lists only 667 souls in this family. Does that refer to a slightly less evil cousin of Mammon? Nope, just a good old-fashioned accounting error. Sometimes coincidences do happen. As Rick

Sanchez is fond of saying, "There's a lesson here, and I'm not the one who's going to figure it out."

DEBATE VII

Is Satan Chemosh?

Dante's Opening Statement: Satan is the Moabite God Chemosh

Whoever Satan is, he should be powerful.

Hold that thought.

The *Ketef Hinnom* is thought to be the oldest surviving fragment of Biblical text. It dates back to the 6th or 7th century BCE.

As far as Bible stuff goes, that's just about as old as it gets... unless we look outside the Bible.

Allow me the pleasure of introducing you to the *Mesha Stele*. It's a vertical stone block inscribed with some squigglies that happen to be a Moabite language. It details the accomplishments of one king of Moab, Mesha. King Mesha of Moab had a god that he worshiped and built a sanctuary for: Chemosh.

The *Mesha Stele* is dated to 840 BCE. That makes it far older than any fragments from the Bible.

But the ol' Steely Mesha doesn't just talk about Chemosh. Yahweh, God of Israel, gets a shout-out too. As it turns out, Mesha gives the counter-narrative to a battle described in 2nd Kings chapter 3.

The story from Mesha's perspective, goes like so:

> "And Chemosh said to me, Go take Nebo against Israel, and I went in the night and I fought against it from the break of day till noon, and I took it: and I killed in all seven thousand men, but I did not kill the women and maidens, for I devoted them to Ashtar-Chemosh; and I took from it the vessels of [Yahweh], and offered them before Chemosh."

It's a simple story. Moab vs. Israel. Moab wins and gets Israel's stuff. According to the *Mesha Stele*, the record is clear:

Chemosh: 1
Yahweh: 0

Surely the Biblical narrative spins it (or unspins it) the other way, right? You'd think so...

The Biblical version has a lot more juice to it. There are more moving parts and it's... well, it's a little bit muddier and harder to summarize than its Moabite counterpart. Mesha wasn't the type of fella to overstay his welcome: "ME, MOAB KING, BASH ISRAEL. TAKE STUFF. ME WIN. ME LIKE CHEMOSH." There's not a lot of subtext there. 2nd

Kings, on the other hand, could conceivably just be subtext; there's much more drama at play.

The Bible tells it this way:
Israel and Judah are split up. Moab was supposed to give Israel 100,000 lambs a year, but after Israel's king dies, the Moabites think they can play fast and loose with the new guy in charge. Turns out, new guy king, Jehoram, doesn't like that. But he is unsure of Israel's ability to bring the hammer on Moab. So he calls up his not-so-friendly neighbors, the kings of Judah and Edom, to form a triumvirate to take down those lamb-hogging Moabites. Before Judah's king, Jehoshaphat, agrees to the pact, he makes sure Elisha, the coolest prophet in the land, gets in some prophecy from Yahweh. Begrudgingly, Elisha calls upon God. Yahweh gives this word:

> *'You shall not see wind or rain,*
> *but that streambed shall be filled with water,*
> *so that you shall drink, you, your*
> *livestock, and your animals.'*
> *This is a light thing in the sight of the Lord.*
> *He will also give the Moabites into your hand...*
> 2 Kings 3:17-18 ESV

He goes on to make some specific prophecies about felling trees and taking names. Those things happen, but in the end, the result is the same as Mesha recounted. Chemosh wins.

So why does this matter (aside from the Bible

getting some outsider archaeological street cred)? The day of battle is recounted in Kings with a glancing reference to Chemosh. It almost serves as a mirror to the *Mesha Stele*. Almost. There is one difference in how the two narratives play out. Not a difference. That's not right. There's a detail; a big detail missing from the Stele.

> *When the king of Moab saw that the*
> *battle was going against him...*
> *he took his oldest son who was to reign in his place*
> *and offered him for a burnt offering on the wall.*
> *And there came great wrath against Israel.*
> *And they withdrew from him and*
> *returned to their own land.*
> 2 Kings 3:26-27 ESV

Great wrath. That wasn't in God's prophecy. And how is this *great wrath* brought about?

Magic.

Mesha slaughters his son like a lamb. He goes full Abraham. FULL ABRAHAM! Abraham didn't even go full Abraham. More striking than the sacrifice itself is its effectiveness.

What entity can win battles after being sacrificed to?

Chemosh gets eight other shout-outs in the Old Testament, which is a good deal for a foreign deity. Aside from being the Big Boss of the

Moabites, Judges 11 insinuates that he's also the head honcho of the Amorites. There are also some fragmented references to "Ashtar-Chemosh" from the Ancient Near East. Scholars suggest that the hyphenated name is similar to the "Yahweh-Elohim" double name of God that arises in the Biblical text on a few occasions. But Ashtar, or Ashtaroth, is referenced 12 times in the OT, associated with various "foreign gods" of the nations surrounding Israel. So, the deeper we look into the issue, there appears to be the God of the Jews and the God(s) of the foreign nations in the Ancient Near East. These foreign gods often seem the same, as if they're the same god cavorting around the region with a handful of different names. Perhaps that god's name is Chemosh.

Chemosh beat Yahweh when Mesha cut open his son for his deity. What conclusion can you possibly make besides this being an emanation of the supreme counterpart to God?

Chris's Opening Statement: Satan is not Chemosh
You're right, Dante. There is a lot of subtext to the 2nd Kings story. There's a ton of moving parts here. I'm a tad disappointed in you because you left out the best part of the story. When the Israeli king goes to Elisha for a word from God, his response is AMAZING.

Elisha said to Israel's king,
"What do we have to do with each other?

Go to your father's or mother's prophets."
Then Israel's king said to him,
"Don't say that, because it is the Lord who
has brought us three kings together—
but only to hand us over to Moab!"
Elisha said, "I swear by the life of the
Lord of heavenly forces,
the one I stand before and serve if I didn't
care about Judah's King Jehoshaphat,
I wouldn't notice you or even look at
you! Now bring me a musician."
While the musician played, the Lord's
power came over Elisha.
2nd Kings 3:13-15 CEB

Elisha proceeds to utter his prophecy while the harpist is playing! He's spitting mad fire bars over the ancient equivalent of a DJ. Get ready for a crazy mixtape from ya boi Elisha!

In all seriousness, though, what's Elisha's beef with King Jehoram? The only reason he jumps on the beat is out of respect for the king of Judah. Elisha doesn't like Jehoram, and for a good reason.

Jehoram comes from a long line of terrible kings in Israel. It all began some 40ish years before with his grandpa, King Omri. At this point in their history, Israel is more divided than ever. Not only had they split with Judah, but they also were split into two factions over who the next king should be. Omri kind of kills his competition, and so he takes the throne. 1st Kings gives us a summary of his time as king.

> *Omri did evil in the Lord's eyes, more evil*
> *than anyone who preceded him.*
> *He walked in all the ways and sins*
> *of Jeroboam, Nebat's son,*
> *because he caused Israel to sin.*
> *They angered Israel's God, the Lord,*
> *with their worthless idols.*
> 1st Kings 16:25-26 CEB

That's all we get on Omri's rule. After him comes his son Ahab, who is even worse than his daddy. Next, Ahaziah reigns for a few years with nothing super special happening. Then comes his brother, our man, Jehoram. Jehoram is better than his dad and his grandpa, BUT not much. So, when Elisha tells the king to ask for a prophecy from the idols of his parents, it makes sense. His family line has disavowed Yahweh and clung to worthless idols. Just a cursory reading of the last half of 1st Kings and the first half of 2nd Kings gives us the idea that God is pretty pissed off with this family line.

All this is to say, it wouldn't come as a surprise if God were to use Moab to bring judgment on Israel. God uses foreign armies all the time in the Old Testament to punish Israel for forsaking Him. That is if that's even what's happening in this story.

Verses 25 and 26 give us a portrait of Israel

whooping Moab. I mean, they are just crushing Mesha in this fight. Then comes the bit where Mesha goes FULL ABRAHAM, and, by your argument, wins the day. This all hinges on verse 27, where it says:

> *And there came great wrath against Israel.*
> *And they withdrew from him and*
> *returned to their own land.*
> 1st Kings 3:27 ESV

That's the ESV translation, which is what you are quoting. The ESV is a quality Bible translation, but even quality translations can leave some interpretation to the reader. Here, however, is a direct interpretation from Strong's Hebrew to English:

> *And there was indignation great against Israel,*
> *so they departed from him to [their own] land.*
> 1st Kings 3:27 Strong's Hebrew

It reads a little funny because it doesn't adhere to English grammar rules, but it makes some things a little clearer. By this account, Israel seems to leave the battle by their own accord. Other translations like the CEB confirm this:

> *As a result, outrage was expressed by Israel.*
> *So they pulled back from Moab's king and*
> *returned to their own country.*
> 2nd Kings 3:27 CEB

In his commentary on this passage, Matthew

Henry says that king Mesha did this:

> "To terrify the besiegers, and oblige them to retire. Therefore he did it upon the wall, in their sight, that they might see what desperate courses he resolved to take rather than surrender, and how dearly he would sell his city and life. He intended hereby to render them odious, and to exasperate and enrage his own subjects against them. This effect it had: There was great indignation against Israel for driving him to this extremity, whereupon they raised the siege and returned."

By this understanding, Mesha isn't a victor in this fight; he's a deranged loser driven to extremes by his enemies who leave him with nothing left. But what about the old Steely Mesh? It's older than any of our Biblical texts, and it is a victory by Mesha's account.

We don't know much about the Moabite culture. Everything we know is either from Biblical support or the Mesha Stele; it's all we've got. The Stele is 34 lines, which is pretty long for an ancient stone inscription compared to other sources. So, we can draw a few more truths from it. Let's look at the first few lines from Mesha.

> "I am Mesha, son of KMSYT (Kemosh[-yat]), the king of Moab, the Di-
> -bonite. My father was king of Moab thirty years, and I reign-

> -ed after my father. And I built this high-place
> for Kemosh in QRH ("the citadel"), a high place
> of sal-
> -vation because he saved me from all the kings,
> and because let me be victorious over all my
> adversaries. Omr-
> -i was king of Israel and he oppressed Moab for
> many days because Kemosh was angry with
> his
> land. And his son replaced him; and he also
> said, "I will oppress Moab". In my days he spoke
> thus.
> But I was victorious over him and his house."
> (Mesha Stele lines 1-7)

Okay, the first thing to note, Mesha had the same problem 4th grade Chris had with English. My words were always too big and I never planned right, so I had to add the dashes and finish the line below it. Maybe I was following along the ancient Moabite tradition of writing, and I deserved better grades!

Anyway, according to Mesha, Israel and Moab's strained relationship goes back to the reign of King Omri! Wait, I remember Omri! Do you? He was that evil king in Israel's history who killed his competition and set up a bunch of idols. He was also the grandfather of Jehoram. Wait a second! Mesha says he fought Omri's son, not his grandson.

What gives? Does the Bible recount this story

wrong? I mean, first off, it lists the wrong king as fighting Mesha, and then it provides us the incorrect outcome too? Is 2nd Kings just full of lies? Maybe. But then again, maybe not.

What if, and hear me out now, the Mesha Stele and 2nd Kings 3 are recounting different battles.

Whoa, full stop.

We know that Moab borders Israel just to their south. Moab was kind of a part of Israel for a time. As the Biblical account goes, their founding father is one of the sons Lot has with his daughter. Yeah, it's a weird story, but we don't have time for it here. Moab goes on to become a nation all their own, but they are a Semitic people.

Throughout the Old Testament, Moab and Israel's relationship is good at times and bad at times. Moab harbors David when he is on the run from King Saul, but later, David lays waste to the Moabite country. In Judges, Moab conquers Israel for a time, and eventually, they revolt against them. The most famous women's bible study character, Ruth, was a Moabite herself!

These two countries have a long history, and a lot of it is bloody. So, if these two battles described here seem different, maybe that's because they are. Given Mesha's description of the event, we know two things about his battle. It happens around the same time he assumes the reign of Moab, about 30 years. Also, he fought against Omri's son, who the Scripture tells us is Ahab. What do you know, Ahab would be ruling under the same timeframe Mesha gives us!

Now, is there a Biblical battle that connects Ahab and the Moabites? Not really. Ahab's reign is more focused on a war with the country of Aram than Moab. We know, though, that there is political tension between Ahab and Moab because right at the start of 2nd Kings, when Ahab dies, it tells us that Moab also revolted. We don't get any more information than that. But, we don't need much more information than that. We know Ahab was a terrible king in God's eyes. Even the description in the Stele of Mesha about taking off the "vessels of Yahweh" tells us that Ahab had built idols and broken God's commandment not to make graven images.

Maybe the order from Chemosh to Mesha isn't Satan trying to overthrow God, but God using a foreign power to punish a terrible king. Perhaps we don't get the same battle as described from Mesha's view because the Biblical writers thought we didn't need it. Maybe this final battle in 2nd Kings 3 is the win for Israel that the text implies it to be. One thing is for sure, Chemosh isn't an all-powerful counterpart to God, and he also isn't Satan.

Dante's Rebuttal: Divine Wrath Says it All

You sir, are trying to throw sand in my eyes. It won't work. I'm like Jean Claude Van Damme in *Bloodsport.* I'll land my roundhouse kick despite your vision-altering dust spray.

Your 'other battle' theory of the *Mesha Stele* is provocative. I'll give you that. But it's beside the point. Ellicot's commentary of verse 3:27 gets us to the crux of the matter:

> *"And great wrath fell upon Israel. This phrase always denotes a visitation of Divine wrath. (Comp. 2 Chronicles 19:10; 2 Chronicles 24:18.)...as the present writer understands the words of the text, they rather indicate that the object of the dreadful expiation was attained, and that the wrath of Chemosh fell upon the Hebrew alliance. It is certain that belief in the supremacy of Jehovah did not hinder ancient Israel from admitting the real existence and potency of foreign deities."*

The inquiry is as simple as this: did divine wrath fall on Israel because of the Moabite sacrifice?

The text, as is argued above, leans toward yes. Even if you think it's more likely that the answer is no, it can't be ruled out. If that's the case, is there any example of non-Yahweh wrath appearing in history stronger than that of Chemosh? If we limit ourselves only to the Biblical texts, then I'd wager the answer is no.

Chemosh and his divine wrath are the most powerful adversaries to God in Scripture. It stands to reason then that Chemosh is most worthy of the prize of being called Satan.

Chris's Rebuttal: Chemosh Isn't Who We Think He Is

You're going to make me say it aren't you? I hinted at it before, but fine, I'll just come out and give my full theory so you can call me a heretic.

Are you ready?

What if Chemosh isn't Satan...

...because Chemosh is Yahweh.

Dante's Rebuttal: Say What?

Uh... Lucy, you got some 'splainin to do!

Chris's Rebuttal: Chemosh as Yahweh Isn't Heresy

Okay. But I warned you.

To understand this theory in total, we need to look at another story. Unfortunately, it's one of the messiest and most confusing in all the Scripture—the story of Balaam and Balak.

If those names don't ring any bells right off the bat, that's okay. They occupy a small percentage of the book of Numbers, and as I said, things get messy. Balak is a king over the nation of Moab, and the Israelites (led by Moses) are headed his way with an ax to grind. Balak realizes there is no way for him to win this fight, so he decides to appeal to the gods for a favor. He seeks out a prophet in his country named Balaam and offers him a grand reward for cursing the Israelites.

So, a few things to keep in mind. Balaam isn't an Israelite. At best guess, he's a wandering prophet living on the outskirts of Moab and is likely a Moabite himself. Balaam refuses to go with Balak's messengers because the Lord tells him not to. They repeat this dance a few times. Eventually, the Lord changes his mind and lets Balaam go with the men under one condition: he can only speak the word the Lord gives him. After some donkey hijinks that aren't super pertinent to our story happen, Balaam arrives at Balak's door.

Immediately, Balak asks Balaam to curse the incoming Israelite army. They build an altar and Balaam begins praying. God tells Balaam to bless the Israelite people instead of cursing them, and he does. This ticks the king off. Thinking a change of scenery will help, they go to a cliff overlooking the Israelite camp.

The same thing happens two more times. Balak wants a curse, and God won't allow it. Frustrated, the king yells at Balaam:

I summoned you to curse my enemies,

> *but now you've given a blessing these three times.*
> *Now get out of here and go home.*
> *I told you I'd greatly honor you,*
> *but the Lord has denied you any honor.*
> Numbers 24:10a-11 CEB

While it is massively confusing that God keeps changing his mind in this story, there is a lot of subtext that can help us understand our 2nd Kings passage better. I always come away with one central question from this text: who does Balak think Balaam is talking to?

If you want to curse a people, it's a pretty silly idea to go to the god of that particular people and ask for woe to befall them. But a straight reading shows that's precisely what Balak is doing. He shouldn't be surprised at all when Balaam refuses to curse the Israelites.

Allow me an assumption. I don't believe Balak thinks Balaam is asking Yahweh for favors, at least not at first. Balak presumes his prophet will inquire of Chemosh.

There are two Hebrew words used to talk about God in this passage: *elohim* and *yahweh*. Almost every translation renders *elohim* as God and *yahweh* as the Lord. We know that *yahweh* is God's unique name when talking to Moses, but the word *elohim* is more generic. It's a title given to any being of might and power. It is used to talk about false gods just as much as it is to speak about Yahweh.

I'm not suggesting that two gods are duking it out in this passage. What I think is noteworthy is that Balak seems to always refer to God in this passage as *elohim*, whereas Balaam refers to God as *yahweh*. The only time Balak calls God by name is in that last verse I quoted where he says, "the Lord (*yahweh*) has denied you any honor." What I am suggesting is that these two guys have a significant communication problem.

Thanks to the Mesha Stele and other archaeological finds, we know the Moabites worshipped Chemosh, likely as far back as the founding of their nation. But, like many nations around them, the Moabites were polytheistic. They believed in a lot of gods. It's why there is a prophet of Yahweh wandering around their country. In fact, Scholar Nissim Amzallag claims that "the Edomites, Kenites, Moabites, and Midianites all worshipped Yahweh to one degree or another."

But again, it seems like a bad idea to get the main god of the group of people you are trying to curse to rain down fire and brimstone. Balak's multiple attempts and usage of the word *elohim* all lead me to conclude that he thought he was asking a different god at first, until he fails and has his Miranda Hillard moment; "Ah!! Yahweh?!? Yahweh!?! Oh my god! The whole time? The whole time!?!? THE WHOLE TIME!?!?"

Now bring that back around to the Mesha Stele. It's not crazy to say that God uses other nations against Israel all the time. It's what half of the prophets are talking about in their books. God uses Assyria, Egypt, and Babylon, so why not Moab? What if Yahweh is masquerading as Chemosh during the Mesha Stele battle, and that's why Moab wins? Like we talked about, the Israelites certainly were doing some evil things that needed correcting. Often, God's correction comes in the guise of foreign nations. It isn't heresy to believe God can use these nations either, even if they don't completely understand who they are working for.

As for our battle in 2nd Kings, I still believe it's a different battle. Sure, Ellciot's commentary says that the Israelites are showing proof of belief in other gods. Why can't that still be Yahweh acting under the name Chemosh? Matthew's commentary explained that God's anger would burn against the Israelites for pushing the king to go FULL ABRAHAM.

You say Chemosh's wrath opposes Yahweh, and thus Chemosh must be Satan. I say Yahweh's wrath opposes Israel, and Satan is nowhere to be found here. The record is clear:

Yahweh/Chemosh: 2
Satan: 0

DEBATE VIII

Is Satan Lilith?

**Dante's Opening Statement: Satan
is Adam's First Wife**

*Thus it is written,
"The first man Adam became a living being;"
the last Adam became a life-giving spirit.*
1 Corinthians 15:45 ESV

Paul, in various ways, claims that Jesus is the second Adam. That's a weird concept. Ricky Bobby told us that "If you're not first, you're last." According to Ricky Bobby, Jesus is last. That's weird. But what about Eve? Do women get a second Eve?

No.
Well...
Maybe?

Maybe Eve is the second Eve. Satan is the first.

The idea of an Eve before Eve may sound like it's out of left field, but I'm not inventing sliced bread here. The idea has been around for at least a millennium. C.S. Lewis' White Witch in the chronicles of Narnia was an evil Eve like character named Lilith, by the by. But let's not get ahead of ourselves just yet.

Let's talk about gender, shall we? The topic's been boiling on the hot stove for a while—time to throw in some potatoes and make a feast.

Jesus says that God is spirit (John 4:24). The Torah agrees:

> *God is not man, that he should lie,*
> *Or a son of man,*
> *that he should change his mind.*
> Numbers 23:19 ESV

When the Sadducees try to catch Jesus in a theological trap, he responds (Matthew 22:30) by stating that angels aren't given in marriage, implying that they're not sexual beings in the way that we are.

BuT GOd iS a BoY! THiS IS blASpHeMY!
I hear your stammering.

God is spirit. The Hebrew word for spirit is gender-inclusive. It has boy and girl parts! Its Greek counterpart is neuter. No gender. Yes, God the Father is always referred to in masculine terminology. So is Jesus. But the Holy Spirit? Not so much.

Croatian-American theologian-extraordinaire,

Mirsolave Volf, wrote in his exemplary book, *Exclusion and Embrace*, that "We use masculine or feminine metaphors for God not because God is male or/and female, but because God is personal (p. 170)." As early as the 2nd century, church fathers were equating the Holy Spirit as an emanation of God's wisdom. Wisdom, in Jewish texts (including Proverbs!), is often portrayed as a person. Not only is Wisdom conveyed as some sort of individual, she's also consistently referred to as a girl. A hot girl. Super good-looking. Fine as hell.

John Milton, in Paradise Lost, wrote of the angels:

> "For Spirits when they please
> Can either Sex assume, or both; so soft:
> And uncompounded is their Essence pure,
> Not ti'd or manacl'd with joynt or limb,"
> Book I, lines 424-426

No manacles for them. Sounds like BDSM is off-limits for angel-folk. No *Fifty Shades of Gray* for them fellas. That's a black and white issue, thank you ma'am!

The point in all of this is simple: Satan can be a girl if (s)he pleases.

If we rationally examine what we know about Satan, the Lilith badge, particularly the idea that Satan may be feminine, will show itself to not be as out of left field as it first appears to be.

Let's start simply: Was Satan (whoever he/she is/

was/will be) created?

Chris's Rebuttal: Genesis Gives No Answer on "Pre-Creation" Ideas

This is perhaps a more difficult question to answer than it might appear. Unlike every superhero and villain, Satan doesn't get an origin story. The Biblical narrative focuses on the account of Creation and how God interacts with said Creation. The only problem is that we get very little information on pre-creation. We don't get a scene of God creating Satan or even the angels in Heaven. Honestly, I think that is purposeful. The Biblical narrative doesn't seem to be super concerned with answering questions that fall outside the realm of Creation. Sure, angels and demons enter the scene and exit, but only as side characters. So, the question becomes, is it fair to ask a question that the Bible doesn't try to answer?

This isn't to say that we can't possibly take a guess. Psalms 8 tells us that God made humans "a little lower than the angels." The psalmist seems to imply the idea that angels are created beings. At the same time, if Ezekiel 28 is about Satan, then it is pretty obvious.

You were in Eden, God's garden.
You were covered with gold and every precious stone:
carnelian, topaz, and moonstone;
beryl, onyx, and jasper; lapis lazuli,
turquoise, and emerald.

On the day that you were created,
finely crafted pendants and
engravings were prepared.
Ezekiel 28:13 CEB

Declaring Satan as an uncreated being also presents several logical problems for us. If God doesn't create Satan, then did something else, or someone else, create him? If so, does that mean there is a realm the Almighty can't control? While I'm not convinced that a comprehensive theology can be drawn on things outside of Creation, I will yield to your question that Satan must, in some way, be created.

Dante's Rebuttal: The Lack of a Satanic Origin Story Means Something

If Satan is created, then the question arises; when? The dual accounts of Creation in Genesis (chapters 1-2:3 and 2:4-3:24) don't give angelic creation even as much as a wink. Perhaps the fall of the angels is a tale that God's stricken from history. Yet, when we dig into the creation accounts, we can begin to feel the poetic pull of Genesis more and more. There are small steps everywhere that seem to be skipped over. For instance, there is no mention of a ceremony of any sort commemorating Adam and Eve as married. Despite that omission, Genesis 2:25 states that "the man and his wife were both naked." Perhaps the Garden of Eden story is much like Hebrew genealogies; it is not meant to be read as a comprehensive history. Instead, the story has chosen its beats purposefully. Some parts are left on the cutting floor.

By late antiquity/early medieval time period, the myth of Lilith was fully realized and propagated amongst various Jewish groups. Her name was commonly portrayed as a demoness that snatched away certain infants. She appears to have been the SIDS explanation back in the day. Her name shows up on pots and plate shards, almost always as a spell or prayer to ward off the evil witch-demon.

The *Alphabet of Ben Sira*, a document dating somewhere between 700-1000 CE, explores the origin story of Lilith for us. Lilith is portrayed as Adam's first wife, however, she apparently wasn't a happy bride. Lilly (or would her nickname be Lithy? Ithy? Lil Ith X?) runs away from her one and only beau. Her reason? She only wants to lay "above Adam, not below." That's right. The first couple in human history broke up over sex positions. She storms out of Eden only to be caught by God's angels. Somehow, they concoct this weird deal. Lilith gets to stay alive and murder newborn infants for eternity, but in return the angels get to kill 1,000 demons every day. You'd think they would have run out of bad guys to slay by now. In order for a child to be secured against the wiles of Lilith, the house that holds the infant needs to have three names written down on an amulet:

Senoy, Sansenoy, and Semangelof. These three dorky names were apparently the angels in charge of medicine. It seems kinda similar to Catholic patron saints... or names of forgotten Hobbits.

Sure, this bonkers story shows up waayyyy after Genesis is written. But fear not, the name Lilith wanders about in the Dead Sea Scrolls as a demon! That puts her at least into the BC era.

Oh, and did I mention... she's in the Bible too! Isaiah gives her a shout-out!

> *And wild animals shall meet with hyenas;*
> *the wild goat shall cry to his fellow;*
> *indeed, there the night bird settles*
> *and finds for herself a resting place*
> Isaiah 34:14 ESV

Did you see that? No. You didn't. Why? Because our translator friends that devised the English Standard Version (ESV) decided to translate the Hebrew word "Lilith" as "night bird". I think they just threw their hands up and decided to keep this little passage all about animals.

Shifting gears for a sec, let's look at the etymology of the word "Eve".

Adam is just the Hebrew word for man. So, the first man created went by the name "Man". You'd think Eve would be the Hebrew word for "woman". Not so fast. The Hebrew word for "Eve" is "*chava*", which happens to be a cognate to the Hebrew word for live, *"chaya"*. So, essentially, Eve means life. That's nice.

No one knows exactly what Lilith means (although the Akkadian word "Lilitu" means spirit or breath), but the word for serpent is... *Chiva*. Eve (*Chava*) is tempted by (*Chiva*). Hmm...

One of the oldest stories in the world (one that predates our written records of Genesis by a thousand years minimum), tells the tale of Inanna, the goddess of Uruk. She wants a tree in her garden cut down. But there's a problem. A snake and a "Lilith" are hanging out in the tree's branches. The goddess calls upon the hero Gilgamesh to chop down the tree. Ol' Gilly kills the snake, but Lilith flies away. Why does she fly away? The text treats her as a bird (I see you ESV translators!). Some might even call her a "night bird". Notice: in this small story, one of two villains is killed. The snake is defeated, but the bird flees to come and wreak havoc another day. The Genesis account includes several of the same elements that this Gilgamesh story does, only with a bonus Lilith. Why are there so many Biblical parallels except this one?

Here goes the theory: Satan is female. He is she. He is Lilith. Hebrew culture, however, as a patriarchal society, couldn't stomach a female adversary to God. Tablet shards from the 10th century before Christ already show us that some Ancient Near East groups worshiped the goddess Asherah as a wife of Yahweh. Perhaps by stripping Lilith's identity out of Satan, God and/or the ancient Hebrews were trying to safeguard their people from being seduced by Satan's story.

Chris's Rebuttal: Ben Sira and John Milton are The Worst

I must say, your theory reminds me of a pastrami sandwich. It's as holy and as cheesy as the swiss one traditionally puts on it. Plus, like the sandwich, it isn't enjoyable.

As I stated before, I believe Satan is a created being, but just because I think he is created doesn't make him Lilith anymore than it makes him Adam. There are no shortages of Lilith stories throughout history. That is, except in the Scripture, where there is indeed a sizable Lilith shortage. But we'll get there.

First, let's talk about the *Alphabet of Ben Sira*. There are two possibilities regarding this work. As you described, the first is trying to give us a better picture of why there are two different accounts of creation in Genesis. The line of thinking goes something like this; there are two accounts of God making humanity, so either Genesis contradicts itself, or there's another woman in Adam's life!

Those options are a false dichotomy. Things are often a lot grayer than they appear. Christianity has no shortage of explanations for why the

Genesis accounts differ. For example, as early as the fourth century, the church father Gregory of Nyssa proposed a simple solution. Greg saw the first account as dealing with God creating the cosmos on a macro level, and the creation of humanity in Genesis 1 is God's grand blueprint for humanity. It's the idea of humanity being constructed "in His image". While Adam and Eve factor into that creation story, the idea is bigger than that. It's all of humanity being conceived by God and set within their proper place among creation.

The second account, says Gregory, is God coming down into His creation to begin crafting it. It's God getting in the mud and muck and creating the first of this important species.

While I love that explanation, the more likely scenario is that two different people wrote these accounts. Despite what your pastor may tell you, Dante, Moses probably didn't write every word in Genesis. He probably didn't *write* any of it. Moses *may* have said the stories found in the book, but they were likely written down long after his passing by various scribes. The book of Genesis is more akin to a compilation of works than a single written piece. Given that the language changes substantially between Genesis 1 and 2, it's not crazy to assume this is the same story by two authors. Whatever the answer, it is odd that Lilith makes no appearance in either.

We don't have to accept the question that Ben Sira is forcing us to ask in his work. What's more, we have good reason to be skeptical of Ol' Benny in the first place. As you said, the *Alphabet* was likely written around 1000 CE. As a whole, the work contains 55 stories. Each one corresponds to a letter in the Hebrew alphabet, kind of like a medieval *A is for Apple* book. We don't know much about the motive for its writing, but we do know its contemporary rabbis largely ignored it. If this work is supposed to reveal the creation story's missing link, you'd think the Jewish community would have held it in some esteem, but they don't. According to Janet Gaines Howe, this has led many scholars to the belief that "Ben Sira's tale is in its entirety a deliberately satiric piece that mocks the Bible, the Talmud, and other rabbinic exegesis." Unlike what you'd expect from serious rabbinical work, Benny likes to mock the heroes in the Old Testament.

There is, however, another work from the same time as Ben's *Alphabet* that is held in higher esteem, and that's *The Zohar*. *The Zohar* is a sacred text by the Kabbalists, a medieval school of Jewish thought. The Kabbalists consider *The Zohar* as sacred as *The Talmud*. Within this work, we see that God creates the first human, not as two creatures, but as one with two genders. One side is male; one side is female. God then saws the creation in half, creating Adam and, you guessed it, Lilith.

The story goes down similar to the *Alphabet*; Lilith doesn't want to be under Adam, so God creates Eve. When Lilith sees her rival clinging to Adam, she flees. Here's where the story gets both weird and exciting. Lilith goes on to meet up with Satan, called Samael, in *The Zohar*. The two enter into an unholy marriage, and God is so concerned that they will pop out demon offspring like rabbits that He castrates Samael. Lilith, unable to satisfy her desires with Satan, decides to get off with men while they sleep. Hey, I said it got weird.

The Zohar sees Satan and Lilith as two different entities. As you've already explained, the oldest tale in history also sees two evil figures; the serpent and the nightbird from *Gilgamesh*. This shows us again a clear distinction between two hostile forces. The Hebrew Scriptures make no mention of Lilith except for that one pesky reference in Isaiah.

Your passage isn't the "gotcha!" moment I think you were hoping for. The only specifics we get about Lilith is that she lives among the desert creatures. Remember *Gilgamesh*? The Lilith-bird thing flies away after Gilly kills the serpent. She flys away "into the desert". Isaiah is written around 740 BCE, and there is no doubt that he was familiar with ancient stories from other cultures, such as *Gilgamesh*. Heck, read all of Isaiah 34. It's a warning to God's people not to associate with the Edomites, for they have incurred His wrath. Much of Isaiah deals with the Israelites being warned against entangling themselves with those who worship foreign deities. Is it a stretch to think that Isaiah's mention of Lilith reminds the people that these ancient deities, like Lilith, are no match for Yahweh?

Where does that leave us? Perhaps an enormous hole in your pastrami sandwich of non-sense is the issue of angel genders. Boy, oh boy, I never did think I'd be writing these words, but here it goes...

Angels are dudes.

I know, I know, that's not super PC of me, but bear with me. The Hebrew and Greek words for "angel" are always masculine. Whenever they show up to folks in the Scriptures, they are always guys. I make no qualm that God's Holy Spirit and the Wisdom of God are feminine, but angels are dudes, at least functionally within Scripture.

Let's not forget that Genesis 6 gives us a pretty clear picture:

> *In those days, giants lived on the*
> *earth and also afterward,*
> *when divine beings and human*
> *daughters had sexual relations*
> *and gave birth to children.*
> Genesis 6:4a CEB

From a purely physiological and functional standpoint, whenever angels are in physical form on the earth, they have penises.

"BuT MiLtON SaId AnGeLs CaN hAvE eItHeR pEnIseS Or VaGiNaS" I can hear you squealing back already.

Look, let's get this straight. I love *Paradise Lost* as much as the next guy, but we should hardly consider John Milton an authority on anything regarding the creation story, but especially when it comes to sex. Milton had several agendas in his work, but none more evident than shock value to his contemporaries. Milton's use of sex in his work is an excellent example of modern-day trolling. He disagreed strongly with religious zealots who wanted to ban sexuality in all its forms. So, he strives to show that sexuality can be a good thing (as seen in the Garden of Eden sex scene) and also a terrible thing (as seen later after Eden is closed and Adam and Eve have a lustful sex scene).

That's all well and good, but man, did he go a little far in his exploration of those ideas, namely with Satan, who rapes his daughter Sin and bears a child named Death. Milton played *really* fast and loose with the creation account. He wanted to shock and offend, and boy howdy, did he, but we can't use him to draw a definite stance on the gender of angels. We just can't.

So who is Lilith? If the authoritative ancient sources are to be believed, clearly not Satan.

Dante's Rebuttal: What About Asherah?
I think you just solved Satan's identity for us. Who is he? He's Lilith's husband, Samael!
Done and done.

But wait just a second here, big fella, let's hold the phone on all this genderizing of angels. Yes, God the Father is referred to exclusively as male in the Bible, and Jesus incarnated as a man, but God the Father is something above and beyond gender. Jesus tells us himself in John 4:24, *God is spirit, and those who worship him must worship in spirit and truth.* Likewise, when speaking of the angelic realm, Jesus says in Matthew 22:30, *At the resurrection people will neither marry nor be given in marriage; they will be like the angels in heaven.* Angels, it would appear, are not made for marriage.

If angels are not made for marriage, then what's a bad angel going to do? Probably try to get himself hitched. Or perhaps I should mind my pronouns and say "herself".

On a jar in a place called Kuntillet Ajrud, a desert land just south of modern-day Israel, in the Sinai, an inscription reads, "Yahweh of Samaria and his Asherah".

Painted alongside the inscription are two figures, arms intertwined, with one of them sprouting a very large frontside. No shrinkage here. Asherah is a Canaanite deity that's referenced over 40 times in the Old Testament. Every time she is lambasted, and her worship is strictly forbidden.

Asherah was the Israelites' forbidden fruit.

Angels are, presumably, spirit beings. I'd argue then that they can likely take the forms they want. We know Satan is against Yahweh. His aim is something akin to undermining everything God does. So then, why not get the people to worship you, and claim yourself as God's bride?

Lillith and Asherah have this in common: they are the rejected wives of famous male rulers. If Jesus is a man, wouldn't it make sense that Satan would choose to appear as a woman?

Chris's Conclusion: Scripture Isn't a Battle of the Sexes

That's it, you brilliant white man, you've solved it! You've discovered the secret Biblical narrative no one else has. The long-hidden message of good versus evil is simply a battle of the sexes! It's nothing more than a bad episode of *I Love Lucy* with a marital dispute at its core.

Is that the best we can do? Man good, woman bad?

It seems to me that this explanation of Lilith, and ultimately Satan, doesn't square well with Scripture, and it's for the same reason you already stated. God isn't gendered. This idea isn't some new age, progressive, "everybody gets a trophy nonsense". It is orthodoxy at its finest. As you stated before, God is spirit, and apparently, in the spiritual realm, angels do not need to marry. But the gendering of God goes so much deeper than these two statements.

Let's start with Jesus. Sure, He is born a dude, but we find Him describing Himself in feminine terms a handful of times.

> *Jerusalem, Jerusalem, you who kill the prophets*
> *and stone those who were sent to you!*
> *How often I have wanted to gather your people*
> *just as a hen gathers her chicks under her wings.*
> Luke 13:32 CEB

Why would Jesus compare Himself to a mother hen in a culture that was so male-dominated? It certainly didn't help any of His claims at authority, and He could have used an analogy of a father animal with a similar effect. But He chooses to identify with the feminine here.

Let's talk about the Holy Spirit now, you know, the often forgotten bit of the Trinity. Much of the early church has a peculiar idea about the Holy Spirit. They refer to it as a *"her"* in many of their writings, including: Origen, Jerome, and Epiphanius. You may say to me, "Well, what do a bunch of dusty dead dudes know about the Holy Spirit anyway?"

First off, don't be rude to the church fathers, Dante. That color doesn't look good on you. Second, without these dusty old dudes, the church wouldn't have much theology related to the Holy Spirit. See, the Spirit is a less present being in the Scripture than I think we'd like to admit. Almost all the doctrine we hold to now about God in three equal persons is scarce in the New Testament and instead was developed by the men you just verbally assaulted.

These guys were connected to Jewish culture and understanding in a way we could only hope to imagine. Because of that, they saw the Holy Spirit as the personification of Wisdom in the Tanakh. As you mentnioned earlier, Jews believed Wisdom was a hot woman, and her personification is visible in passages like Proverbs 3:13–18, 4:5–9, 7:4–5, 9:1–6, and Job 28, to name a few. This personification of Wisdom made the early Jewish-Christians look at the Holy Spirit not as a man, but as a woman!

Still not convinced? Let's look at one more example, often ignored, by Paul.

> *There is neither Jew nor Greek;*
> *there is neither slave nor free;*
> *nor is there male or female,*

for you are all one in Christ Jesus.
Galatians 3:28 CEB

Sure, this passage doesn't show us God in correlation to gender, but it does teach us that gender isn't as important to God as we may think. It suggests that whether one is male or female has no bearing on the innate worth a follower of Christ has. In short, it shows us that God encompasses all genders. No one is disqualified in God's view due to their gender, and we shouldn't be surprised given that God Himself, or Herself, seems fine to identify as both genders.

Could it be then that Lilith and Asherah aren't condemned because of their gender, but instead because they, like any other slew of made deities, are false idols? If we are saying that Satan can be a false idol, I'll certainly agree with you. But Satan as the literal figure Lilith embroiled in a battle of the sexes against a male counterpart doesn't make sense.

Dante's Conclusion: The Evidence is Everywhere!
I said it once, I'll say it a thousand times: man good, woman bad. I mean, if you switch the letters in Hitler and turn the 'L' into an 'S' and turn 'A' into 'E', that spells Ishtar, the Babylonian goddess! And Stalin, well, if you spell his name in Cyrilic Cyrillic, it looks like: CTALNH, which is kinda unpronounceable like the Lovecraftian god Cthulhu, who, frankly, is clearly a female

monster whose existence is meant to mock male impotence. So, I mean, like, all the stars are aligning to make my point for me. And let us not forget! All the dinosaurs at Jurassic Park are females! What does that tell you????

And I quote from that glorious 1993 film:

> Dr. Ian Malcolm: *God creates dinosaurs, God destroys dinosaurs. God creates Man, man destroys God. Man creates dinosaurs…*
> Dr. Ellie Sattler: *Dinosaurs eat man….. Woman inherits the earth.*

I rest my case, and the case of all MANkind.

DEBATE IX

Is Satan Death?

Dante's Opening Statement: Satan is the Idea of Death

A long time ago, in a world we can no longer comprehend, a little girl, suddenly pushing air out of her lungs and tossing her wet limbs to-and-fro in confusion, was born. They took her. They. Straight from her home. Straight from her mama. She was flayed alive. Some say her little jaw was unhinged and broken. She was born only to be sacrificed in this way.

She descended into hell... or, at least, the underworld. There. In the darkness, she took for herself a husband. He, and her beside him, ruled the underworld.

Her name was Mictecacihuatl. But that's not what they call her anymore. She's known more commonly as "Nuestra Senora de Muerte". Our Lady of Death. Among certain Catholics, she's deified as a powerful saint.

On the surface, the story is easy to comprehend. It's a simple syncretism of faiths. The Aztecs had a renowned goddess of the underworld. The Catholics also had a goddess of a sort: the Virgin of Guadalupe. The Virgin is otherwise known as Mary, the Mother of God. Jesus' mama. When two faith traditions butt heads a little convergence is bound to happen.

Exhibit A: Christmas in December when scholarship tells us Jesus was likely born in Spring. Exhibit B: Easter. The word Easter comes from the Germanic goddess Eostre who the pagans celebrated in early springtime.

It stands to reason, then, that the reverence of Santa Muerte is merely a missing-link sort of animal; some monster of cultural evolution and nothing more.

Here's the chink in that armored idea: Cortes conquered the Aztecs in the 16th century, and Santa Muerte has only taken root in the 21st century. Sean Kirkpatrick, summarizing the issue for Crisis Magazine, wrote, "Nearly five centuries later, the Bony Lady of Death has supplanted the pregnant Lady of Life and drawn ten million back to the shadow." In fact, the cult of Santa Muerte is, by some accounts, the fastest growing religion in the Western hemisphere.

Why?

Because she wins.

Look at the Old Testament. Is there nary a mention of the afterlife in the Torah? No. That's why the Sadducees (the ruling class of Jewish priests in the 1st century CE) didn't believe in any life after death. Moses went and "slept with his fathers." In the histories, all the accounts of Jewish kings, every last one of them, whether they had been bad boys or princely angels, died and "slept with his fathers."

Now, before you get that bulbous brain of yours humming, let's talk Sheol.

Sheol is the Jewish afterlife. But what is it? Nothing. It's sleeping. It's nothingness. Death is finality. Death is no longer functioning. Death is the end. Sheol is rest. Rest in Sheol. R.I.S. Or perhaps RIPIS: Rest in Peace in Sheol.

After wrestling with his own Jewish roots, Sigmund Freud concluded that evolutionary mechanics pointed to man ultimately evolving out of religion. Why? Because, as The Internet Encyclopedia of Philosophy summarizes Freud's thoughts: "Religion has failed to deliver on its promise of human happiness and fulfillment; it seeks to impose a belief structure on humans which has no rational evidential base but requires unquestioning acceptance in the face of countervailing empirical evidence."

Santa Muerte has been called the cult of the cartel. There seems to be a strong undercurrent of acceptance and worship within the drug smugglers and gun-toters south of the border. Why? Death is real to them.

You don't get it. Not yet.

In your heart of hearts, you still believe you'll live forever in this life. Something in you thinks you'll go on and on. You won't. You'll die. The cartel knows this better than you, better than I. They stare death in the face every day. That's why they know her name.

There is no heaven in the Torah because there is no need for it; heaven is a place on earth. Or so the Jewish nationalists thought. But then they lost. And lost. And lost. Then they hungered. Then they suffered. And suffered. And suffered. The whole of Israel, much like Job, finally reached a point where even if they got their kingdom back, even if everything was put back together, it wouldn't be enough. Justice and happiness could never be found on earth. There's just too much PTSD floating in all of us. So the brain takes the logical next step.

You can't get salvation here… so maybe it's over there… on the other side of death.

And so Heaven is created.

Why does Santa Muerte exist in the 21st century? Why is she exploding on the scene as the cool, new, hip artist? Two reasons:

-1) Death always wins.

-2) Some folks know they're too broken for heaven.

Heaven is a great help for those who believe they'll gain an entrance ticket. But what if you've done bad things? So many bad things. What if you've killed people? Children. Better yet, what if you've watched these things happen in front of your eyes since you were a baby yourself? So much so that you can't even imagine a good place? What then?

Answer: you join the winning party.

Satan has always been the rebellious winner.

They say Jesus defeated death. Why then is death still going?

Chris's Opening Statement: In All Satan Tries, He Fails

A *Vanity Fair* article, written just after the 2020 election results, features an interview with talk show host Stephen Colbert. Much of the report focuses on Colbert's relationship with President Joe Biden. Colbert reminisces about a conversation he and Biden had several weeks before the election when he asked Biden what it would mean if he lost. The former Vice President replied, "Maybe I'm a bad candidate."

Colbert illustrates the difference between President Trump's approach to campaigning and Biden's, and along the way, he compares how that approach mirrors Christianity. Trump *has* to win, or his failure and loss will mar everything he built up over the four years. But, as Colbert notes, Biden can *accept* the loss because he knows that it won't be the end of him.

You may be asking what this has to do with Christianity. The talk show host points out that both candidates claim to follow Jesus, but only one's attitude is reflective of the cross. Colbert calls Biden's answer victorious, and says, "It shows enormous confidence. The message of Christ isn't that you can't kill me. The message of Christ is you can kill me, and that's not death."

Loss, on any level, is a complex emotion for humans to comprehend. No doubt, the death of a loved one or close friend can break even the strongest of us. Looking around us, it certainly feels like death is consistently winning. Then again, we aren't alone in feeling this way.

Consider the early church for a moment. We like to romanticize their lives because they had just witnessed God resurrecting Jesus and defeating death! But their lives after the resurrection were far worse off than they were before. Take the apostles; out of the twelve, only John died naturally. Every other Apostle met a grizzly end. James is beheaded. Peter is crucified upside down. Thomas gets pierced by four spears. Matthias gets burned to death. Several more met various endings by stabbing, crucifixion, and torture. Why would a religion whose head honchos all wind up with their heads in baskets be worth following?

Yet, the church persisted.

The writer of Hebrews gives us a glimpse into the lives of those who chose to follow the apostles:

> *Others were tortured and refused to be released*
> *so they could gain a better resurrection.*
> *But others experienced public shame by*
> *being taunted and whipped;*
> *they were even put in chains and in prison.*
> *They were stoned to death, they were cut in two,*
> *and they died by being murdered with swords.*
> *They went around wearing the*
> *skins of sheep and goats,*
> *needy, oppressed, and mistreated.*
> *The world didn't deserve them.*
> Hebrews 11:35b-38a CEB

What a terrible pitch for gaining memberships! Why would anyone want to be a part of anything that would put them in the path of gruesome ends? Surely things should be getting better for Christians eventually, right? Yet almost a hundred and fifty years after the death of Jesus, we find a recounting of a renowned Christian bishop named

Polycarp.

No, Polycarp is not a Pokemon. That's Magicarp. Held in Christian tradition to be just below the Scriptures, *The Martyrdom of Polycarp* is an extra-biblical text that gives us a fascinating insight into the Roman world's persecution. The text was written to encourage believers in the church of Smyrna and begins like this:

> "All the martyrdoms which God allowed to happen (remember that the devout will ascribe all things to his sovereignty) were blessed and noble. Who could not admire their honor, their patience, their love for the Lord? They were whipped to shreds till their veins and arteries were exposed, and still endured patiently, while even those that stood by cried for them… In the same way, those who were condemned to the wild beasts endured dreadful torture. Some were stretched out on beds of spikes. Others were subjected to all kinds of torments, all in the Devil's attempt to make them deny Christ."
> (The Martyrdom of Polycarp 2)

This is a horrific history, but it's that last bit that I want to focus on. The writer tells us this was all part of the Devil's scheme to get believers to deny Christ. Satan's playbook against the people of God seems to be pretty straightforward: torture, harm, and kill. Yet, in the face of all this death, Polycarp remains unwavering.

The Roman officials capture Polycarp and drag him out to a large crowd to make a spectacle of his death. The Proconsul attempts to get him to repent to the Roman gods, but Polycarp refuses. Then the official threatens to throw him into a pit full of wild animals, but ol' Poly welcomes the beasts. So, in a fit of rage, the official threatens to burn him alive. Poly's response?

"Why are you waiting? Bring on whatever you want." (The Martyrdom of Polycarp 11)

Aside from Polycarp giving a baller answer to a government employee, the Procouncil, in his fury, lights a fire and throws Polycarp into it. But a miracle happens! The fire doesn't burn his body, and the official has to demand his soldiers stab Polycarp inside the fire with a dagger. Only then does Polycarp die.

What we would expect as a sad occasion among the Christians quickly turns to a celebration. They gather up his bones and throw a party to celebrate his homecoming! What kind of crazy cult is this?

The early church viewed torture and death as tools of Satan, for sure. But the crazy thing is that they knew death wasn't the end for them. To them, Jesus had defeated death, but that didn't mean death wasn't a part of life. Jesus' resurrection reclaimed all things, including death.

It's the same hope that Joe Biden sees in Jesus; death is not the end. A loss is not final. All things will be made new again. It's why Stephen Colbert can look Biden in the eyes and ask, "Are we going to be alright?" and be meant with a resounding "Yes. We are."

Perhaps the death cult of Mexico isn't far off. They worship death because they see death as the winner, and maybe in our earthly existence, that is the case. But Jesus calls us beyond death and back into life, and that promise is for all of humanity, even the most broken ones. Satan cannot be death, for death is not a person; it's a tool that he uses to discourage us. But Jesus has reclaimed that tool, and now He uses it to welcome us home.

As the writer of *The Martyrdom of Polycarp* says, "In all that the Devil attempted he failed, thanks be to God."

Dante's Rebuttal: The Narrative May Not Be True

I agree that that's the narrative. Christianity blossoms when we're persecuted. But how true is that narrative?

The book and subsequent film by Martin Scorcese, *Silence*, proffers a troubling counter-narrative. The story fictionalizes the true story of Christian missionaries, and Christianity in general, persecution into oblivion in medieval Japan. They tortured Christ off the island for hundreds of years. With Japan still having a Christian witness of less than 1% of the population, it appears the strategy worked.

And then there's the other angle: Christianity (and all other religions) flourish when it comes with a sword. Would Islam be alive today if Mohammad's followers didn't spread the religion with righteous zealotry throughout Arabia? Would the African continent still be following their tribal gods if it weren't for Westerners enslaving their populations in the name of the Lord?

Folks worship Santa Muerte because she wins, baby.

For every saintly example, I can find a counter-punch. Oh yeah, and I don't have to bring politics into it either, Jerkface.

Chris's Rebuttal: Death Will Be Defeated

I'll concede that Tertullian's often quoted phrase "the blood of the martyrs is the seed of the church" doesn't always ring true. It's a broad brush generalization of an idea that looks at many different contexts. But then again, so is the idea portrayed in Scorcese's film.

Silence does a lot of things right. It shows the commitment of early missionaries in Japan while also humanizing the brutality the Japanese officials deal out. However, it is set in the 1630s and largely overlooks that Christianity had been in

Japan for 100 years prior and possibly as far back as the 13th century. That's a lot of history, and a lot of context, to simply ignore.

Some of the first Christians to land in Japan were Portuguese Catholics. Unfortunately, they were mistaken by much of Japan as another eastern Indian religion. This mistaken first impression didn't go well for the Christians, as the Japanese had a mixed history with India and their beliefs. But hey, you can recover from a first impression, right? As more missionaries came over, they brought with them the Jesuits, which is the group *Silence* follows.

The Jesuits were tolerated at first by the government because they brought trading opportunities to the merchants. However, the Jesuits soon began to demand that the merchants pressure those around them to convert to Christianity to continue their trade relations. These merchants were some of the most respected people in Japan, so naturally, they were a great source of converts for the missionaries. The Jesuits would then demand that their converts begin living in Western ways, giving up their names for Portuguese Christian ones and changing other aspects of their culture. Of course, this angered Japanese officials, who began to lash out at these missionaries. Why wouldn't they? Japan had a long and rich culture, and family legacy was highly valued to them. It's no wonder the

Jesuits attempted assimilation didn't work. The Japanese would eventually close their borders to all missions and trade work for 250 years, hence why it remains one of the most unreached places globally for the Gospel. But there are other examples we can look to that show us the same thing.

In America, a very similar thing happened. English and Spanish missionaries attempted for a long time to assimilate the Native Americans into Western-style Christianity. Yet, it ultimately failed. The missionaries tried everything they could think of to convert the Natives. They even went so far as to steal children away from their homes and drop them into institutes to raise them as Christians. Today, only 10% of Native Americans claim Christianity as their religion, and they aren't even isolated from the Western world. The example of Native Americans and Japan show us that conversion tactics based on the sword rarely work, even if Christians are persecuted in the process.

What of Africa, though? Americans enslaved nearly the whole continent, and today the black church is a thriving part of the Christian ecosystem. Well, I believe that's primarily due to Christianity being present in Africa for hundreds of years before missionaries attempted to subjugate the continent. Heck, Africa has as long of a Christian tradition as most European countries. Tertullian himself was African. In Ethiopia, the church likely existed as early as the first century! Though Christianity was used as a hammer against the African people, they had a purer form before the white man ever got there.

There is one example, though, that doesn't fit with this theory. At least on the surface. In Mexico and parts of Latin America, Europeans forced their Christianity on those subjects. For centuries, it largely worked. Mexico used to be the most catholic nation in the world. Yet, in recent years, Christianity has been declining. Enter, Santa Muerte.

The worship of "Holy Death", as it's translated, is essentially a recent development. It has roots in ancient Aztec worship but wouldn't be what it is today without another religion; Christianity. See, Christianity in Mexico and Latin American became obsessed with the glorification of Mother Mary. Mary, for many, represented healing and protection. But soon, syncretism began. Merge ancient Aztec death worship and the worship of Mary, and "Our Lady of Death" is born.

I believe that the cult of Santa Muerte would not be what it is today without those first Spanish missionaries. They brought Christianity to the nations by force and coercion, and so it's no wonder that a religion born out of death ends up being one that worships it. Today, we see the fruit of what those missionaries planted, and it's rotten.

So, did Satan corrupt Christianity in all these cultures? Is he death personified? I don't think so. We humans often screw up the way of Jesus we claim to be so gung-ho about following. Instead of preaching the way of death to life, we bring death with us, and it's no wonder the nations are confused.

Regardless, there is one final nail in the whole "Satan is death" coffin. While I'm not one for reading too much into Revelation as a book predicting the future, there are a handful of passages that are about events to come. Specifically, these passages tend to happen toward the end of the book.

John the Revelator introduces a whole bunch of characters throughout the book. Jesus is there, and Satan is there too, often depicted as a giant red dragon. Early on in the book, however, we meet the four horsemen of the apocalypse. What do you know, they all have different functions and names. The final one is the most important one for us.

> *When he opened the fourth seal,*
> *I heard the voice of the fourth living*
> *creature say, "Come!"*
> *So I looked, and there was a pale green horse.*
> *Its rider's name was Death, and the Grave*
> *was following right behind.*
> Revelation 6:7-8 CEB

Death personified literally shows up in the narrative. The cult of Santa Muerte didn't invent the wheel on this one; Scripture beat them to it by almost two millennia. Interestingly enough, it's not Satan. Satan seems to have no control or command over Death. It's the Lamb who opens the seals that brings death, not the dragon. But it's the final prophecy about the two that shows us they are different entities.

In chapter 20, we get one of the few predictions of our future that Revelation offers, and it's glorious:

Then the devil, who had deceived them,
was thrown into the lake of fire and sulfur,
where the beast and the false prophet also were.
There painful suffering will be inflicted upon
them day and night, forever and always.
Then I saw a great white throne and
the one who is seated on it.
Before his face, both earth and heaven fled away,
and no place was found for them.
I saw the dead, the great and the small,
standing before the throne, and scrolls were opened.
Another scroll was opened too; this is the scroll of life.
And the dead were judged on the
basis of what was written
in the scrolls about what they had done.
The sea gave up the dead that were in it,
and Death and the Grave gave up the
dead that were in them,

and people were judged by what they had done.
Then Death and the Grave were
thrown into the fiery lake.
This, the fiery lake, is the second death.
Revelation 20:10-14 CEB

Satan gets thrown into the fiery lake, and so do Death and the Grave, but at separate times. John makes it clear, the devil will be defeated, but Death and the Grave still have a part to play in God's plan before their final defeat. That part, giving up those who have died.

That might not seem important but think back to Colbert, "The message of Christ is you can kill me, and that's not death." Revelation is predicting just that. Jesus will free the dead because for those who fall asleep in Him, death is only a doorway. It's a transition, a temporary holding cell that Jesus will break open. The greatest irony of it all? Death isn't immune to death.

Revelation calls it the second death. The casting into the fiery lake. Surely, this second death can't be supported anywhere else in Scripture. Enter Jude:

They are damned, for they follow
in the footsteps of Cain.
For-profit, they give themselves
over to Balaam's error.
They are destroyed in the uprising of Korah.
These people are like jagged rocks just

> *below the surface of the water*
> *waiting to snag you when they join your love feasts.*
> *They feast with you without reverence.*
> *They care only for themselves.*
> *They are waterless clouds carried along by the winds;*
> *fruitless autumn trees, twice dead, uprooted;*
> *wild waves of the sea foaming up their own shame,*
> *wandering stars for whom the darkness of*
> *the underworld is reserved forever.*
> Jude 11-13 CEB

Jude is speaking of false teachers who are trying to sway believers. Notice, among his many sick burns, Jude calls these people "twice dead". Does Jude hate these folks that much that he wishes them dead twice? No. Because the first death isn't the end in Christianity. The image of Santa Muerte isn't the last word. Death, the Grave, and Santa Muerte will all be defeated and given over to the second death.

That is the ultimate hope of Jesus Christ.

DEBATE X

Is Satan the Prince of Rome?

Dante's Opening Statement: We're on a Boat

Remember Prince? And remember when he changed his name to that symbol thing? The only words we were given to identify him was, "The Artist formerly known as Prince". That was weird. And then, one day, he went back to being called Prince.

Satan is the "Prince of the Power of the Air". At least, I think that's a safe assumption based on Paul's words:

> *And you were dead in the trespasses and sins*
> *in which you once walked,*
> *following the course of this world,*
> *following the prince of the power of the air,*
> *the spirit that is now at work in the*
> *sons of disobedience--*
> Ephesians 2:1-2 ESV

Now, as the title of this here chapter elucidates,

I'm arguing that Satan is a Prince over Rome... but then again, maybe he's the Prince of America, or of Wales. The Prince of Wales. Is that Harry? Anywho, Satan is the Prince of [insert country of desire here].

That sounds weird. I know. But here you are... on my boat. We're going into a tunnel now. It's dark. I start singing.

Round the world and home again
That's the sailor's way

God has two families. A heavenly family. An earthly family.

Faster faster, faster faster

The work of redeeming creation is a work of redeeming both the heavens and the earth. This is why Christ says, "Behold I am making all things new." It's also why John the Revelator says that there will be "new heavens and a new earth" in the end. Both parts of creation need recovery, need salvation from death and decay.

There's no earthly way of knowing
Which direction we are going

The imprint of God's two families are all over Scripture. Sons of God. Sons of Man. Two groups. Two delineations.

We first hear about these two families in Genesis

6. The "Sons of God" take a look at the "Daughters of Man" and think to themselves, "I want me some of dat ash!" It appears that it's primarily this transgression, the procreation of "Nephilim", that angers God so much.

He devises a plan to wash it all away in a global flood.

There's no knowing where we're rowing
Or which way the river's flowing

God, obviously, relents in his plan of complete destruction.

The "Sons of God" show up again at the beginning of Job. The story says that the "Sons of God" were in heaven presenting themselves before God. Satan is listed as being among them. Satan is a Son of God. As the story unfurls, Satan's taunt is accepted by God. God chooses his human to win a bet against an angel: son of god vs. son of man.

Is it raining, is it snowing
Is a hurricane a-blowing

Over and over again, the prophet Ezekiel is referred to as the "Son of Man". Why him?

Much of the book of Ezekiel follows the presentation of visions given to Ezekiel by an angel. The angel constantly refers to Ezekiel as a "Son of Man". That's the delineation. The angel sees him as something different than himself. We humans are fundamentally made of different stuff than angels.

The redemption plan for Man, made in God's image, dates back to the serpent's curse in the garden. Perhaps the redemption of the heavens took a little bit longer to commence. Now turn your eyes to the Tower of Babel.

Not a speck of light is showing
So the danger must be growing

Through the foggy lens of Genesis' rushed early history, sometime after the flood, we can spot a people who have become hubristic. They build a tower. Right, right, we all know this part. God confuses their speech. Languages are created. But look closely. Two little elements of the story give us both insight and confusion. First, when God sees the tower, he says, "Come, let us go down and there confuse their language" (Genesis 11:7a). Why the "us"? Who is the "us"? Then, post-tongue confusion, the story of Babel ends with this line:

And from there the Lord dispersed them
over the face of all the earth.
Genesis 11:9b ESV

He dispersed them. Separated. Divided.

If that was all there was on the Babel front, well then, it'd just serve as a little hors d'oeuvres. But pastor and smarty-pants theologian, Michael Heiser, found some connecting tissue over in Deuteronomy. Near the conclusion of Moses' final book, we get this:

When the Most High gave to the
nations their inheritance,
when he divided mankind,
he fixed the borders of the peoples
according to the number of the sons of God.
Deuteronomy 32:8 ESV

According to Heiser, what we have here is the beginning of God making his name great by humbling himself. Thousands of years later, he'll turn up the humble-ness dial with the incarnation of a Jewish man from Galilee. Here, at this early stage of human history, God the Father is humbling himself among the Sons of God.

The theory is simple: God divided the world into precincts, putting Sons of God in charge of them. The next verse tells us what He took.

But the Lord's portion is his people,
Jacob his allotted heritage.
Deuteronomy 32:9 ESV

God lowered himself to the level of the angels. He took a small people and made them the most important nation in human history.

The Sons of God are gods. The Sons of Man are men. See how this works yet?

Are the fires of Hell a-glowing
Is the grisly reaper mowing

Without Psalm 82, this theory falls flat. What can you say, though, to this passage? It exists. You can't look away. It's too clear; its waters, crystal.

> *God has taken his place in the divine council;*
> *in the midst of the gods he holds judgment:*
> Psalm 82:1 ESV

God has a divine council. He calls the other folks in that council "gods". The psalm goes on to criticize these other gods. What for? Judging unjustly. God then speaks to his council:

> *I said, "You are gods,*
> *sons of the Most High, all of you;*
> *nevertheless, like men you shall die,*
> *and fall like any prince."*
> Psalm 82:6-7 ESV

They are "sons of the Most High". Who is the Most High? It can't be anyone other than Big-G God himself! But isn't Jesus God's son? Christ is supposed to be the only begotten! What the heck did we memorize John 3:16 for, if not to know that Jesus is the only son of God!?

Notice: although they are not men, they will die like men.
Notice: although they are in heaven, they will fall like princes.

> *Yes, the danger must be growing*

Another agonizing passage comes to us in 1 Kings. God uses his council for evil. Breathe it in. Every word.

> *And Micaiah said, "Therefore hear*
> *the word of the Lord:*
> *I saw the Lord sitting on his throne,*
> *and all the host of heaven standing beside him*
> *on his right hand and on his left;*
> *and the Lord said, 'Who will entice Ahab,*
> *that he may go up and fall at Ramoth-gilead?'*
> *And one said one thing, and another said another.*
> *Then a spirit came forward and stood*
> *before the Lord, saying, 'I will entice him.'*
> *And the Lord said to him, 'By what means?'*
> *And he said, 'I will go out,*
> *and will be a lying spirit in the*
> *mouth of all his prophets.'*
> *And he said, 'You are to entice him,*
> *and you shall succeed; go out and do so.'*
> *Now therefore behold, the Lord has put a lying spirit*
> *in the mouth of all these your prophets;*
> *the Lord has declared disaster for you."*
> 1 Kings 22:19-23 ESV

Angels aren't just sitting around. They are a part of God's council. Some rule over peoples and nations. God's angels are gods.

Don't believe me?

In the book of Daniel, the prophet recounts a time

when he fasted for over three weeks in mourning. Finally, on the 24th day, an angel appears to him. The shiny angel-fella seems apologetic to Daniel as he gives the reason for his delay in coming to the prophet:

> *"Fear not, Daniel, for from the first*
> *day that you set your heart*
> *to understand and humbled yourself before your God,*
> *your words have been heard, and I have*
> *come because of your words.*
> *The prince of the kingdom of Persia*
> *withstood me twenty-one days,*
> *but Michael, one of the chief princes, came to help me,*
> *for I was left there with the kings of Persia,*
> *and came to make you understand what is to happen*
> *to your people in the latter days."*
> Daniel 10:12-14a ESV

The angel is stopped, forcibly it sounds, by "the prince of the kingdom of Persia." Persia, at this point in civilization, is the biggest friggin' empire the world has ever seen. Persia is the big boy on the playground. No one's bigger. So, this little angel fella can't overcome the opposing force. He's outmatched. It takes the archangel Michael himself to free this guy from the clutches of the Persian prince.

Notice: Michael is identified as a "chief prince".

Heaven is ranked.

Yes, the danger must be growing
For the rowers keep on rowing

Enter Jesus. Who is he? Son of God or Son of Man?

Fascinatingly, Jesus repeatedly refers to himself as a "Son of Man", not as a "Son of God". Why? I think the answer is simple: he knew that once he did what he was going to do, the easiest answer to his identity would be to say he was never really human. He was something else. A spirit, maybe. An angel, perhaps. Jesus is laser-focused on telling everyone he can that he is a man: flesh and blood. Add to that, Christ's miracles point easily enough to the fact that he's also a Son of God. Jesus lets others call him a Son of God, never rebuking them for the claim. See, he's also building relationships in his ministry. He is like you. A Son of Man. One of us.

It is in Jesus that God's two families, Heaven and Earth, are rectified.

Now, let's pivot to Rome.

If the Prince of the kingdom of Persia is the bigwig god during Daniel's day, and Chemosh, the god of the Moabites, is a son of god and so can manifest his power on earth, then what the heck is going on? What's God's plan for all this spiritual politicalness? In Daniel, we get lots and lots and lots and lots and lots of confusing political kingdom talk. Why is that important? What spiritual significance could that possibly contain? Not much... unless... unless God has plans for the various sons of god ruling as princes.

One last Bible story.
It's a big one.

The temptation of Jesus by Satan.

> *Yes, the danger must be growing*
> *For the rowers keep on rowing*
> *And they're certainly not showing*

Jesus endures three temptations. In Matthew's account, each temptation ratchets up the anxiety and tension. Finally, Satan makes his big sell. He'll give Jesus everything he has, if only Jesus worships him. The prize for the devil is victory without end. God's two families will never be cured of their sickness.

The Gospel of John doesn't include the temptation account. Nevertheless, it does offer us some insight into Satan's identity. Jesus, speaking to his disciples, says:

> *Hereafter I will not talk much with you:*
> *for the prince of this world cometh,*
> *and hath nothing in me.*
> John 14:30 KJV

Satan is the "prince of this world". In first-century Judea, what was the world?

Rome.

Yes, the danger must be growing
For the rowers keep on rowing
And they're certainly not showing
Any signs that they are slowing

Satan did have something real to offer Jesus. It wasn't a forgery.

Dr. Michael Heiser's theory purports a vision of God's movement in time wherein he has chosen to humble himself not just in Jesus, but also in the midst of his heavenly council. By giving the world over to angelic authorities and only taking Israel for himself, God showered himself in humility.

Then Israel was destroyed. Over and over again. Jesus suffered. His suffering, though pitiable and horrible, crowned him in glory forever. God did the same through his grief over Israel's demise.

When Willy Wonka took his crew of wannabe successors through his wondrous boat ride, Veruca Salt, the girl who got everything she wanted, said the only poetic thing she ever would:

Daddy, I do not want a boat like this.

Yes, the danger must be growing.

Chris's Rebuttal: Willy Wonka is a Monster
I've never much cared for *Willy Wonka and the*

Chocolate Factory. Maybe it's because I had the book read to me as a child. Perhaps it's because I saw the horrendous 2005 remake before Gene Wilder's rendition. But, I like to think it's because the ending seems too good to be true.

As the movie winds down, we find Charlie and his grandpa aghast to find out they won't win the prize. Wilder stands from his half desk and screams for them to leave because of a couple of silly mistakes. Charlie's grandpa calls Wonka an inhuman monster as they begin to storm out.

On their way out, Charlie stops and returns the everlasting Gobstopper he stole. Wonka murmurs something about good deeds and immediately changes his mind. Twist reversed. He takes Charlie to the Wonkavader. While soaring high above the town and factory in 70s CGI magic, Wonka explains that he is giving the factory to Charlie. Everything is great! Charlie will be rich beyond his wildest dreams. Cut to credits.

As I said, the ending seems too good to be true. I'm not alone either. In the last few years, theorists have speculated that Wonka is that inhuman monster old gramps calls him just a scene before. See, the movie's events correspond with the passing of the OSHA act in 1971. OSHA is the organization in charge of making sure businesses follow safe practices.

A careful watch of the movie reveals that Wonka

breaks a myriad of codes. One brave theorist went through and found nearly 60 different violations that Wonka would be on the hook for. These violations all come with fines, and he calculated that old Willy would be shelling out 26.1 million dollars a day to keep his factory running under these conditions. To put it simply, the chocolate factory is a death trap. Even the production crew and movie itself were hit with OSHA fines due to some of the ways they handled scenes.

Why offload the factory onto a child? Wonka himself says that an adult wouldn't understand, but maybe the inverse is true. Any reasonable adult would know that this factory is a nightmare that makes the tunnel of terror look like a romp in a garden. A child who knows nothing of OSHA, on the other hand, only sees the factory as a golden ticket to lifelong happiness. The dark truth is, Wonka wants out before an endless string of fines forces him to close his doors. Charlie isn't the best kid for the job or even the most morally sound choice; he's just the biggest sucker. He's a kid born in poverty with no idea the legal trouble he could find himself in as the owner of the Wonka fortune.

The last scene is much more sinister when watching the movie through this lens. It almost sounds like a scene we are already familiar with. Wonka takes our protagonist up to the highest point and shows him the vast chocolate kingdom that can all be his. But it's a lie. Sound familiar?

*Then the devil brought him to a very high mountain
and showed him all the kingdoms of
the world and their glory.
He said, "I'll give you all these if you
bow down and worship me."
Jesus responded, "Go away, Satan,
because it's written,
You will worship the Lord your God
and serve only him."*
Matthew 4:8-10 CEB

Satan promises the kingdoms of all the Earth, but the reality is he's a liar. Jesus flat out calls him the father of lies in John. He doesn't have the authority he claims to. Look no further than Paul.

*Every person should place themselves
under the authority of the government.
There isn't any authority unless it comes from God,
and the authorities that are there have
been put in place by God.*
Romans 13:1 CEB

What shall we assume then? If Satan really rules all the kingdoms of the Earth, does Paul want us to bow to him? Of course not, because Satan doesn't control the nations. A "prince" of something may have some power, but the king will always overrule him. So, when Jesus calls Satan the "prince of this world", it shows us what little power the devil has.

What about this whole council thing, though?

Who are all these dudes hanging out with God making decisions and what not? Could it be that Christianity has a pantheon of gods who rule different nations?

Like you said, your theory hinges on Psalms 82. So, let's take a close look at this passage together.

> *God takes his stand in the divine council;*
> *he gives judgment among the gods:*
> *"How long will you judge unjustly*
> *by granting favor to the wicked? Selah*
> *Give justice to the lowly and the orphan;*
> *maintain the right of the poor and the destitute!*
> *Rescue the lowly and the needy.*
> *Deliver them from the power of the wicked!*
> *They don't know; they don't understand;*
> *they wander around in the dark.*
> *All the earth's foundations shake.*
> *I hereby declare, "You are gods,*
> *children of the Most High—all of you!*
> *But you will die like mortals;*
> *you will fall down like any prince."*
> *Rise up, God! Judge the earth*
> *because you hold all nations in your possession!*
> Psalms 82:1-8 CEB

That word "gods" shows up several times in this passage, and given the understanding you have given us, we should assume that the psalmist refers to the pantheon of lesser spiritual beings who rule the nations. Wait a second; this is all starting to sound familiar. I think I've heard this before somewhere. Let me search for it; it's got to be somewhere. Oh! That's right, here it is!

> "And the Gods took counsel among themselves and said: Let us go down and form man in our image, after our likeness; and we will give them dominion over the fish of the sea, and over the fowl of the air, and over the cattle, and over all the earth, and over every creeping thing that creepeth upon the earth."
> (The Pearl of Great Price, Abraham 4:26)

Yup, you read that right; *"Gods,"* capital G and all. If you are wondering, that's not the Genesis account given in Scripture. Nope, instead, that's part of a reworked account Joseph Smith gave his followers. The Church of Jesus Christ of Latter-Day Saints, or Mormons as they are more commonly known, have a theology that looks frighteningly similar to this Divine Council.

In the creation account in the extra-Biblical work *The Pearl of Great Price*, Abraham explains how the pantheon of Gods came together to create the world and how two separate Gods volunteered to redeem it. Those two Gods are Satan and Jesus. Jesus gets the council's approval while Satan is denied, driving him into a fit of jealousy.

We are making strange bedfellows when we end up on the side of Joseph Smith. So the question becomes, is there something else the writer of

Psalms is getting at? The key to this conversation is the word "gods" in Psalms 82. The original Hebrew word there is *"elohim"*. That word can refer to God, but it is also often used to refer to high-ranking officials within a governing system. Think of it like the British colloqualism "lord". No one in Britain believes they call someone the one supreme God when they use the term lord. It's a sign of respect for a high-ranking position.

When we take the context of this passage in totality, it makes more sense. God says that he is enthroned above the "great assembly" or "divine council", whatever you want to call it. That assembly is a poetic representation of all the kings of the Earth. God then critiques the kings of the Earth by calling them out for their terrible execution of justice. This is not an uncommon thing in Scripture either. Look no further than; Psalms 2:2-6, Psalms 76:12, Jeremiah 25:17-26, Lamentations 4:12, Luke 22:25, Acts 4:26, and Revelations 6:15. Unjust and wicked kings are often condemned.

The point of Psalms 82 is that God is the only one who renders true justice. This also helps us better reconcile the end of this passage when God calls out the other "gods" but then says they will surely die like mere mortals. They are flesh and blood humans, not some expansive pantheon of spiritual beings.

But you may ask why God uses a plural pronoun during the tower of Babel incident. He does clearly say "us" and not "I". He even does it before then, too, at the very beginning of Genesis when He says:

Let us make humanity in our image.
Genesis 1:26a CEB

Who is this "our" and "us"? For that answer, we turn to the early church. Justin Martyr in the 2nd century claims that:

> "You may not change the force of the words just quoted, and repeat what your teachers assert,--either that God said to Himself, 'Let Us make,' just as we, when about to do something, oftentimes say to ourselves, 'Let us make;' or that God spoke to the elements, to wit, the Earth and other similar substances of which we believe man was formed.'"
> (Dialogue With Trophus, Chapter 62)

Tertullian, when defending against the heresy of Marcion, wrote:

> "If the number of the Trinity also offends you, as if it were not connected in the simple Unity, I ask you how it is possible for a Being who is merely and absolutely One and Singular, to speak in plural phrase, saying, "Let us make man in our own image, and after our own likeness;" whereas He ought to have said, "Let me make man in my own image, and after my

own likeness," as being a unique and singular Being? In the following passage, however, "Behold the man is become as one of us," He is either deceiving or amusing us in speaking plurally, if He is One only and singular."
(Tertullian, Against Praxes, Chapter 12)

Finally, Ireneus says:

"It was not angels, therefore, who made us, nor who formed us, neither had angels power to make an image of God, nor anyone else, except the Word of the Lord, nor any Power remotely distant from the Father of all things. For God did not stand in need of these beings, in order to the accomplishing of what He had Himself determined with Himself beforehand should be done, as if He did not possess His own hands. For with Him were always present the Word and Wisdom, the Son and the Spirit, by whom and in whom, freely and spontaneously, He made all things, to whom also He speaks, saying, "Let Us make man after Our image and likeness;"
(Ireneus, Against Heresies, Chapter 20)

Overwhelmingly, the second-century church fathers saw this as an example of the Trinity. Justin sees this as God talking to Himself, as even we are prone to do. Tertullian sees the three distinct persons of God as giving us a reason for God to "talk to Himself". Ireneus flat out denies that God had created a lower "god" pantheon to rule over humanity. In your defense, Dante, this is one of the main issues the church debated for hundreds of years. The Trinity is a complex concept to grasp. But thousands of men and women before us have devoted themselves to answering this question, and the Protestant position is that God is Triune, not that He created a multitude of gods.

The end of Psalms 82 gives us the last piece of the puzzle when it says, "God! Judge the earth because you hold all nations in your possession." God doesn't take just Israel and rule nothing else; He brings all nations under His authority. Just like Wonka, Satan has no actual claim to the power he grants. And if I know you, DuhduhDante, which I do, you're going to throw this oft-quoted Bible-verse at me next:

> *We aren't fighting against human*
> *enemies but against rulers,*
> *authorities, forces of cosmic darkness,*
> *and spiritual powers of evil in the heavens.*
> Ephesians 6:12 CEB

Why are there so many references and allusions to "princes" and "authorities" in both the New and Old Testament? The answer isn't that there's a celestial hierarchy of demonic spirits earning new ranks with every military coup that takes place in human history. That would be a heavenly bureaucratic mess. Why would God create such a chaotic system?

Paul tells us that God is not the author of confusion (1 Corinthians 14:33). The listed rulers and powers that Paul gives credence to are the very systems of oppression that still bring injustice and calamity to us to this day! Scripture reminds us that when we amass power, we fallen humans create ideologies, alliances, prejudices, and flowcharts that help magnify sin and spread it throughout the world. But I don't need to prove my case in this chapter, just disprove your crazy-go-nuts one! I'll leave it to the Addendum: Systems of Oppression to pontificate further on how God, in scripture, makes us aware of how aggregated human power is against the will of God.

So, that was a lot. Let's review. God is over all. God is Triune. Mormons believe in many gods. Satan is a liar. Willie Wonka is a monster. Check-mate.

Dante's Rebuttal: Checkmate, My Buttocks!
Let's go through your final points one-by-one, shall we?

"Willy Wonka is a monster."
--You are a joyless imp to make such a scandalous attestation! You're a Bible scholar, for Pete's sake. You, more than most, should understand the importance of genre when coming to conclusions about authors' intent. Roald Dahl did not expect

the reader of his marvelous children's book to impute modern hygienic codes into the fabric of his story. It's not about that. Everybody wants to be Charlie Bucket. Let us be the kid that gets what he always wanted! Goodness, Mr. Scrooge! Let Bob Cratchet have the day off, already. Have a heart!

"Mormons believe in many gods."
--Yup. They sure do. The fact that they hold errant views on God should not be weighed in a discussion of whether or not my theory is valid. This is the fallacy of 'guilt by association'. You then double down on the fallacy by saying, "Look at me! Irenaeus and Tertullian are on my side." Oh yeah, well, well… uh… Nic Cage is on MY SIDE! So there! Take that.

"God is over all. God is triune."
--Yup. These are also true facts. I don't think they're relevant to my point, however. God can be over all, triune, and Satan can be the angelic Prince of Rome. Those three statements are not contradictory in any way.

"Satan is a liar."
--Yup. Once again, this is not a contradictory statement. In fact, I'd argue that history shows us that those with titles of power and jurisdiction over territory tend to be liars. What politician isn't a liar? Satan can be a deceiver and a prince.

You took some time to debunk the "Dr. Heiser Psalm 82 Divine Council" theory. As I understand it, your point was

    a) Elohim doesn't always refer to gods, and

    b) God is triune, so therefore the divine council business is silly *Willy Wonka* talk.

To an extent, I agree with you. To steal a phrase popularized by Islam: there is no god but God. That being the case, you can't just toss out the divine council idea because it doesn't fit well into your theological box. We can look outside of Psalm 82 to toss more evidential coals upon your hide.

As I referenced earlier, parallel accounts in 1 Kings 22 and 2 Chronicles 18 show us a potentially disturbing image of God's council. In it, the prophet Micaiah says,

> *I saw the Lord sitting on his throne,*
> *and all the host of heaven standing beside him*
> *on his right hand and on his left...*
> 1 Kings 22:19 ESV

God wants to prevent King Ahab from succeeding at his ventures, so he inquires of his throne room delegation what should be done. One spirit offers to go out and convince Ahab of a lie. God likes this plan and sends the spirit on its way. Is this spirit a member of the trinity? It sure doesn't sound like it.

Throw out Psalm 82 if you'd like. My hypothesis could still stand. God, at certain times, has given authority and power to other spiritual entities. The Prince of Persia episode speaks to this. Oh, and you suggested that "prince" means something lesser than a king. That can be true, but then what do you do with:

> *For to us a child is born,*
> *to us a son is given;*
> *and the government shall be upon his shoulder,*
> *and his name shall be called*
> *Wonderful Counselor, Mighty God,*
> *Everlasting Father, Prince of Peace...*
> Isaiah 9:6 ESV

To say that princes don't have authority is to undermine Jesus' own power, no?

Where's your checkmate now?

DEBATE XI

Is Satan the Winner?

Dante's Opening Statement: Satan Wins
Ezekiel 26 begins with God's proclamation against the nation of Tyre.

> *For thus says the Lord God:*
> *Behold, I will bring against Tyre from the north*
> *Nebuchadnezzar king of Babylon, king of kings,*
> *with horses and chariots, and with horsemen*
> *and a host of many soldiers…*
> *They will plunder your riches and*
> *loot your merchandise.*
> *They will break down your walls and*
> *destroy your pleasant houses.*
> *Your stones and timber and soil*
> *they will cast into the midst of the waters.*
> Ezekiel 26:7,12 ESV

That's all well and good. There are lots of prophecies from Yahweh against rogue nations in the Old Testament. This one in particular, however, has a swift fulfillment.

Three chapters later, in Ezekiel 29, Nebuchadnezzar, that mighty king of Babylon, has laid siege against Tyre.

> *Son of man, Nebuchadnezzar king of Babylon*
> *made his army labor hard against Tyre.*
> *Every head was made bald,*
> *and every shoulder was rubbed bare,*
> *yet neither he nor his army got anything*
> *from Tyre to pay for the labor that he*
> *had performed against her.*
> Ezekiel 29:18 ESV

God specifically noted the riches that Neb and his army would procure from Tyre, and it wasn't nothing. What gives? Is this a mis-prophesied prophecy? The oddity doesn't end there. God works to set things right in the next verse:

> *Therefore thus says the Lord God:*
> *Behold, I will give the land of Egypt*
> *to Nebuchadnezzar king of Babylon;*
> *and he shall carry off its wealth and*
> *despoil it and plunder it;*
> *and it shall be the wages for his army.*
> *I have given him the land of Egypt as his payment*
> *for which he labored, because they worked*
> *for me, declares the Lord God.*
> Ezekiel 29: 19-20 ESV

The simplest reading of the event is to surmise that God didn't quite hit the nail on the head with his ability to see the future. Let's dole out partial credit for knowing ol' King Nebby would invade Tyre, but take some deductions for the lack of loot in the endgame.

What the hell is going on here?

At darn-near the beginning of the book of Judges, an *Apocalypse Now* style book of the Bible that just unravels further and further into blood, sex, and guts the further it goes, this paradox occurs:

> *And the Lord was with Judah,*
> *and he took possession of the hill country,*
> *but he could not drive out the inhabitants of the plain*
> *because they had chariots of iron.*
> Judges 1:19 ESV

Did chariots of iron beat God? What happened to Yahweh's chariots of fire? How is this possible? That's the question, isn't it?

What is possible?

If God predestines the future, then almost nothing is possible. Only one future is ever possible; that which God predestines. This gets into time travel logic real quick, and that Sisyphisian concept is not one I'm eager to climb, so let's keep this as simple and linear as possible, okay?

According to Pastor Greg Boyd, there are 39 Biblical passages where the text explicitly states that God changes his mind, and another 200 where the text implies a Godly change of mind. There's another handful of passages where God expresses being surprised by how events turned out. There are also several instances when God regrets having done something, and dozens of occurrences wherein God tests people to see what the testees will do.

Perhaps God got his prophecy about Tyre a little bit wrong. Does that matter? Does Tyre have any significance or connection to Satan? Yes. It's between the prophecy against Tyre in Ezekiel 26 and its resolution in chapter 29 that we get God's words of condemnation against the Prince of Tyre, and then... the King of Tyre, who was...

> *in Eden, the garden of God...*
> *an anointed guardian cherub.*
> Ezekiel 28:13-14 ESV

The prophecy against the King of Tyre ends as one might expect:

> *You have come to a dreadful end and*
> *shall be no more forever.*
> Ezekiel 28:19b ESV

What if God is wrong about how it all ends? If there's Biblical evidence that God cannot precisely know the future, perhaps Satan can still win. Perhaps Tyre won't be looted after all. Maybe God will throw some Egyptian demon into the lake of fire instead.

**Chris's Opening Statement: Prophecy
is Way More Complicated than
You're Making it Out to Be**

A lot of folks believe they have a good understanding of how Pop music works. Grab a teen heartthrob, throw him in a recording booth, play four chords, add a sick beat, slap some auto-tune on that bad boy, and BAM! Instant chart-topper, right?

Simplification of Pop music has been propagated by many people who often snub their nose at the genre in favor of a "more complex" form of music. But that assumption couldn't be further from the truth.

Pop music is complex. Often, it's just as complex as "technical genres" like jazz. As a prime example, take Lil Nas X's chart smasher *Old Town Road*. At the time of this writing, the song is the longest-running number one song on the Billboard charts. It spent 19 weeks unmoving as the most played song. 19 weeks! For comparison, most songs only make it a week before being knocked off. In fact, only 3% of songs spend more than ten weeks at number one, and *Old Town Road* nearly doubled it.

Most people would tell you that the song is nothing but silly rapping behind bland instrumentals. I don't believe that's a fair criticism of the music, though. For starters, the instrumental samples a different song; *34 Ghosts IV*. It is an instrumental track featuring gloomy banjo plucking by Trent Reznor, the founder of Nine Inch Nails. You know, the guy so prolific that Johnny Cash himself covered one of his songs and called him a "masterful songwriter."

But Lil Nas didn't just steal a hit song. *34 Ghosts IV* was created ten years before *Old Town Road* and had been relatively unknown. Nas also chopped the piece up to emphasize the major aspects of the song instead of the minor focus Reznor originally had. Nas spent, all in all, a lot of work and time to take this obscure deep cut to a number one sensation. Pop music is often far more complicated than it sounds at first.

So is prophecy.

We think of prophecy as being simple; "God said x *would happen*, so x *must happen* or God is wrong." But the term prophecy in the Christian religion is about much more than just predicting the future. A better definition of it is simply having a message from God.

Thumb through the prophets, and you'll undoubtedly find predictions of the future coming from God, but you'll find just as many statements or truths about a nation's current state of affairs. The book of Amos is a fantastic place to see this in action. It includes prophecies about what is to come for the nation of Israel, but there are also passages like this:

> *Seek good and not evil, that you may live;*
> *and so the Lord, the God of heavenly forces,*
> *will be with you just as you have said.*
> *Hate evil, love good, and establish*
> *justice at the city gate.*
> *Perhaps the Lord God of heavenly forces will*
> *be gracious to what is left of Jacob.*
> Amos 5:14-15 CEB

Notice here that Amos does not give a prediction of what is to come. Instead, the Israelites are given the command to love good and hate evil. Their fate is left uncertain. This tends to be more common than we might think; prophecy often doesn't come guaranteed. Depending upon the actions of the people within the prophecy, stuff can change. The best-known example is that of Jonah. Jonah is told to tell the Assyrians to repent or doom will come on them. He runs away, gets eaten by a fish, and then is vomited up. After all that, he goes throughout the Assyrian capital proclaiming God's coming wrath. Something unexpected happens, though, and the people repent. Jonah sits atop his hill, waiting for the promised calamity, but it never comes because God decided to show mercy.

No one understands the Jonah narrative as a "failed" prophecy, even though it's a prophecy predicting a future that never comes to pass. Humanity has a role in the messages God gives, and sometimes that results in different outcomes. Prophecy is more complicated than we tend to think, and our story in Ezekiel may be the next Old Town Road.

What's going on in our story? To start, let's get some background on Tyre. There are two different parts to this ancient city, one on the mainland that consists of suburbs and one on an island just off the coast. Tyre proper is the name Ezekiel gives to the island bit while calling the mainland part "settlements" or "towns". In fact, before talking about the island part of Tyre, God says Neb will destroy with the sword these towns around Tyre.

While we don't know much about the history of the siege against Tyre, we do know that Nebby boy attempted to attack the mainland settlements first. However, upon his arrival, they were found empty because all the inhabitants had sought refuge on the island. What was left of the towns seems to have been destroyed by the Babylonian army. But from there, things get fuzzy.

We know that Babylon's siege of the island of Tyre lasted 13 years, at which point they gave up and brokered a ceasefire. But Tyre was not left unscathed, taking a page out of Aaron Burr's book; old Nebecunezzer might say he "got more than he gave." The King of Tyre was dethroned and killed while Neb set up one of his men as king of the city and likely walked away with revenue from the city's seaports. Nebecunezzer ended up with a pretty good deal despite what Ezekiel would have us believe.

Remember, though, prophecies aren't set in stone and can change. Perhaps our first clue that things weren't going to go down the way God said was the abandoned towns. It turns out telling your opponent what your first move will be doesn't always end well. Ezekiel's prophecy seems to give them the head start they need to leave the town. Add onto that 13 years of unknown history, and you have to admit that a lot of stuff could change.

But all of this is missing the more significant point. Could Satan be the ultimate winner?

The good news is a resounding no. How do I know that? It's not based on some prophecy from Revelation yet to come true, but on the most crucial story that you and I know so well. Satan can't win because he has already lost.

Christ's death and resurrection is the final word. They are the climax of the grand story God is telling. Jesus has won the day, as Paul says:

> *He destroyed the record of the debt we owed,*
> *with its requirements that worked against us.*
> *He canceled it by nailing it to the cross.*
> Colossians 2:15 CEB

The key here is the resurrection. Paul also tells us that if the resurrection isn't true, we must be pitied above all men. But we believe Christ died and rose again, defeating the powers of darkness, and most importantly, Satan himself. Indeed, you wouldn't question or deny the resurrection, would you, Dante?

Dante's Follow-Up: So, What You're Saying Is...
Your argument, if I'm understanding you correctly, boils down to two ideas:
-1) Biblical prophecy serves a different purpose than we generally think it does.
-2) The war is over. Jesus defeated Satan at the resurrection, so there's no hope for Satan.
Is that a fair distillation of your argument, or am I missing something?

Chris's Clarification: Let's See What You Got!
Your summation is a bit reductive. But what the heck, I'm feeling generous today. Take it away, Mr. Stack.

Dante's Rebuttal: Pain Points to Satan's Victory
If Biblical prophecy is not about predicting the future, then what exactly is its purpose?

My favorite scripture passage in all the Bible is the one you just referenced: 1st Corinthians 15. Paul lays it out plainly for once in his life. If Christ isn't resurrected, then we're the scourge of the earth, the most to be pitied.

The hope of the Christian is ultimately as simple as holding to the conviction that death is not the end of us. Our great hope remains that Jesus' resurrection foreshadows our own. Paul says that Jesus is the first fruits of the resurrection. Our resurrections are, presumably, coming next. We are the second fruits.

But...

If prophecy isn't an accurate depiction of the future, then what is? Folks are dying all around us... they haven't woken up yet. I can't feel my Dad's hands. His body is decomposing right now in a box six feet underground. My mother mourns. There's no earthly evidence currently that my father has resurrected. Granted, Paul points towards the horizon for our perfection:

> *Then comes the end,*
> *when he delivers the kingdom to God the Father*
> *after destroying every rule and every*
> *authority and power.*
> 1 Corinthians 15:24 ESV

One of my favorite songs of all time is hardly a song. It's closer to a spoken word poem than it is a song. It's by William Shatner. Captain Kirk. The refrain of this near perfect song-poem is Shatner repeating the ominous line, "It hasn't happened yet."

Shatner reads to the sway of the music:

"When do I feel I haven't failed?
I've got to get it together, man...
I'm waiting for that feeling of contentment
That ease at night when you put your head
down"

Then that ominous line, over and over again:

"It hasn't happened yet"

The rhythm continues as Shatner bellows the last lines before the wretched chorus line takes us away:

"At my age I need serenity
I need peace --
It hasn't happened yet"

You might call ol' Captain Kirk's spoken song just a bit of melodrama. You might.

It happened in 1999. Shatner came home to find his wife at the bottom of their swimming pool. Her death was ruled an "accidental drowning". She'd taken valium with her alcohol that evening.

Some years later, Shatner wrote a poem about finding his wife that night. The poem is set at the moment of discovery. He crystalized the instant for us... or perhaps for himself. The poem ends this way:

"Her body still and blue
Is this what death looks like?

My love was supposed to protect her
It didn't
My love was supposed to heal her
It didn't
You had said don't leave me
And I begged you not to leave me
We did."

Oh, death, where is your sting? That's the line, right? That's what Paul announces and we Christians are called to echo. Can you not feel the sting? Does it not hurt? Does it not pierce your skin like those nails 2,000 years ago? Does death not cause us to suffer?

It does sting, doesn't it?
Doesn't it.

One of my students at the state prison was in jail for raping a tiny child. Rape is always heinous, but rape of a little one... what on God's earth do you do with that? I knew this man. I looked him in the eye every day. I said encouraging words when he did poorly on exams. I celebrated with him when he began to excel at his school work. Was Satan already defeated when he raped that child? It doesn't feel like it.

Judges 1:19 is one of the most disturbing passages in scripture. It stings.

> *And the Lord was with Judah,*
> *and he took possession of the hill country,*

but he could not drive out the inhabitants of the plain
because they had chariots of iron.
Judges 1:19 ESV

The Lord was with Judah, but...

I know that the Bible tells me that the resurrection of Jesus of Nazareth showcased the defeat of Satan and death, but I'm still waiting for death not to hurt.

It hasn't happened yet.

Chris's Reply: I Have No Proof, Only Faith

I, too, feel the sting.

When I was 12, my cousin was shot 23 times and killed in his own home by a bookie he owed a measly $1,000. A year later, my grandmother died slowly at 73 of lung cancer she inherited as secondhand smoke. In high school, a close friend brutally hung himself and was found by his sister. He was followed that year by two other teenagers in my class who also took their lives. To this day, I carry them with me, along with the pain of their loss. I confess I have no platitudes to heal that pain, and I believe it will accompany me, along with countless other traumas, to the grave.

Faith is the reality of what we hope for,
the proof of what we don't see.
Hebrews 11:1 CEB

I hope for an end to my pain. I hope for an end to yours and the whole world's as well. But the fact is I have no proof because I live in the in-between. I live in-between the death of Christ and the final resurrection of the dead. As Shatner said, "It hasn't happened yet."

Why couldn't Judah beat out the rest of the inhabitants? Why do any bad things happen? Maybe it's a paradox of our free will and that of the entire world, playing out in real-time. Perhaps it's because, like us, they lived in the in-between too. I don't know. All I know is that it hurts.

But I believe Christ was resurrected. Because of that faith, I also believe my friend, my grandmother, my cousin, and I will all rise one day. Call it a foolish hope, and pity me if you must, but I have faith that Satan will not be the final winner.

DEBATE XII

Is Satan God?

Dante's Opening Statement: He Built a Boat!

This one guy makes ships. He's good at it. He's a shipbuilder. Presumably, his papa was a shipbuilder, as was his papa's papa.

This fella makes good money from his ships.

One day he hears about Christianity. Naturally, it intrigues him. He quickly falls in love with this Jesus guy. He reckons that Jesus was a good dude. Not just good, but the best. These are the early days of Christianity, so there aren't Bibles thrown around left and right. Our fella shipbuilder receives his puzzle pieces in the mail, one letter at a time.

He learns that Jesus is, in fact, God. He's astonished. Blown away! Petrified, mortified, and… well, convinced! Jesus is Lord. Jesus is King! Jesus is God.

Having read that the rich young ruler didn't give away all his stuff when told to by Jesus, our dear shipbuilder decides to do what he can. He makes a substantial donation to the church in Rome. And I mean SUB-STANT-IAL.

But then our lovely shipbuilder gets his paws on some of the Old Testament stuff. He reads of Yahweh, the vengeful god. Yahweh who tells the Israelites to genocide whole peoples. Yahweh who accepts Jephthah's sacrifice of his daughter. Yahweh who curses and hates and condemns and kills and blames and rebukes and disciplines.

Our shipbuilder is befuddled. How can this be? He makes an effort to read more of the Jewish scriptures. Over and over again, he reads words that don't compute. How could this be the same God who begot Jesus?

There's only one honest solution to come to... the god of the Old Testament is not the same as the god of the New Testament.

Chris's Opening Statement: Yahweh Isn't as Violent or Vindictive as We Think

Your first-year seminary knowledge is rather impressive, my friend, but you've left out some essential details in Marcion's life.

Sure, Marcion could not see a way to reconcile the Gospel accounts with the Tanakh but it's a little more nuanced than you'd like us to believe. It's important to note from the start that he lived in the late first century and the early second century before Christianity had accepted any official canon. It's vital because Marcion would not have simply been able to "get his paws" on a copy of the New Testament, as up to this point, there is no "New Testament".

Yes, the letters and books that make up our current Scripture existed during Marcion's time, but not as a collective work. An early church congregation would likely only have access to whatever copies of letters they were privileged to receive. While we may have access to the entire canon of Scripture at our fingertips today, the early church wasn't so lucky and may only have a fraction of the books that comprise our New Testament. What's more, they may or may not have considered other works as equal to the Scriptures, such as the Shepherd of Hermas or the Gospel of Barnabas. The point is, during Marcion's early life there was no accepted "standard" version of the New Testament like we have now. Some congregations probably differed on what they believed to be inspired in the Old Testament too. The crazy thing is, we have Marcion to thank for our canon.

So, Marcion sees Yahweh as incompatible with Jesus and has likely limited access to the totality of Scripture. What does he do? He goes out and makes his own "official" canon of Scripture using parts of the Gospel of Luke and ten of Paul's epistles. As a result, the proto-orthodox church is forced to do two things: expel Marcion, and devise their own canon.

Remember that substantial donation you're so gleeful that Marcion gave? Upon his expulsion as a heretic, it was returned to him by the church. Now, this is far from the most important point here, but I wanted to note that even a massive amount of money couldn't sway church leaders enough to look away from Marcion's heresy. That's saying a lot.

His ex-communication had a lot to do with that whole "making his own canon" deal. For starters, Marcion heavily edited the Gospel and Epistles he kept, flat out omitting entire sections of Luke that didn't fit within his belief system.

I'll pause here because I can already hear you screaming. "WAIT, Chris!!! Isn't that how all canons are formed? Don't we keep the part we agree with and throw away those we don't?"

Simmer down there, boy. Consider Marcion's attempt to create a canon over and against the creation of the canon we have today. Marcion compiled and edited it all by himself. However, our current canon began to take its shape around 200 C.E. and didn't resemble what we know until the 5th century. That's several hundred years of disagreements and hundreds of people's input on what should constitute the Biblical canon.

Sure, you could look at that and say it's just

the Marcion problem on a larger scale, but where Marci was focused on subtraction, the early church councils seemed more concerned about addition. They didn't omit sections of books because they disagreed with them. They added some passages like John 8, which we are still unsure today if it appeared in the original formation of the Gospel. What you won't find in our Biblical canon are missing sections of books.

All that doesn't answer Marcion's criticism, though, that Jesus and Yahweh are two different gods. It feels a bit silly for me to rehash several thousand years of church thinking on this topic shortly and concisely, so I want to point out one big point I think proponents of this theory overlook.

Yahweh is not the violent, vindictive God that many believe Him to be.

I don't have the time to go through every instance of it in the Old Testament. Still, we often misunderstand the context of many stories and suppose God promotes the violence we read about. I believe the most gruesome parts of the Old Testament come from the book of Joshua. As such, I'm going to focus my concern here. But the same ideas that we will see play out in a moment end up being remarkably similar to almost every other story in the Old Testament. So consider Joshua our microcosm of why Yahweh isn't the vengeful God we tend to think He is.

In her book *A Filipino Resistance Reading of Joshua 1:1-9*, scholar Dr. Lily Fetalsana-Apura takes a fantastic in-depth look at the context surrounding the story of Joshua. While I can't give you every single point she touches on, Fetalsana-Apura sets out to show that we often read Biblical passages from a colonized Western viewpoint. These passages were not written to show a world superpower dominating its enemies. Instead, they flow from marginalized and oppressed people attempting to establish themselves among foreign powers that wish to enslave them. She compares this history with that of her homeland in the Philippines and their resistance to colonial rule based upon Christian teaching. Essentially, Yahweh is not building up a mass army to commit atrocious genocides against the Canaanites. He is providing a way for His people to resist their oppressors. Of Israel, she says:

> "As a part of a national narrative, Joshua must be read in its international context. A small and weak nation, dominated by the great empires of the ancient Near East, Israel expropriated the divine warrior concept against its colonial proponents... In defiance of the empire, Israel claimed to be a people of Yahweh and none other. Leaning on its faith in Yahweh, tiny Israel dared to resist the ancient superpowers. In alluding to war waged and

fought by Yahweh, Israel declared war against colonialism."

Beginning to think of the Old Testament wars in their proper context shows us that Yahweh is not commanding slaughter willy nilly, but as a response to the culture around the Israelites. "*Slaughter*", however, is still not really an accurate word. See, most of the conquest passages within Joshua read like this one:

> *I myself will remove the entire*
> *population of the highlands*
> *from Lebanon to Misrephoth-*
> *maim before the Israelites*
> Joshua 13:6a CEB

Notice that God uses the language "remove" instead of kill or destroy. Add on to that the fact that Israel isn't commanded to do the removing; God will do it. We see God "removing" people all the time, even within Israel! Adam and Eve were "removed" from Eden because of their sin. Cain was "removed" to the wilderness for his violence. It's also not like "removing" the Canaanite people came without warning.

It's easy to forget, but way back in Genesis 15, God tells Abram that he will have to wait for 430 years because the Caananites had not yet exhausted God's patience. They get 430 years to turn to the God of Israel before Joshua and his army get there. God is warning Canaan that they can either face

Him as Savior or as judge, similar to the warning we see reflected in the life of Jesus. Even once Israel gets there, God doesn't allow them to go on a killing rampage. In one of the first battles we see in the book, Joshua is told to have the men march around the city of Jericho for seven days before beginning the invasion.

Look, if your plan for total conquest begins with giving the enemy army seven days to surrender or prepare for your attack, you're doing war wrong. But that's the whole point. God wants to offer the Caananites one final grace, prompting author Preston Sprinkle to say, "God believes, therefore, in preventive wars— wars waged by grace."

The book of Joshua does seem to make a point out of the Israelites "wiping out" several cities and following God's instruction in doing so. This happens six times throughout the book, but none seems more violent than what happens to the city of Ai in chapter 8:

"When Israel had finished killing all the men of Ai in the fields and in the wilderness where they had chased them, and when every one of them had been put to the sword, all the Israelites returned to Ai and killed those who were in it. Twelve thousand men and women fell that day—all the people of Ai. For Joshua did not draw back the hand that held out his javelin until he had destroyed all who lived in Ai. But Israel did carry off for themselves the livestock and plunder

*of this city, as the Lord had instructed Joshua.
So Joshua burned Ai and made it a permanent heap
of ruins, a desolate place to this day. He impaled
the body of the king of Ai on a pole and left it there
until evening. At sunset, Joshua ordered them to
take the body from the pole and throw it down at
the entrance of the city gate. And they raised a large
pile of rocks over it, which remains to this day."*
Joshua 8:24-29 CEB

Yeah, I'll give it to you; this feels like overkill. According to this passage, Joshua and his men kill everyone and then, just for good measure, impale the king's body from a pole in humiliation. I can see why a story like this would turn Marcion's stomach and make him question if Yahweh and that loving Christ were one and the same.

It's important to notice something, though, there is one character absent from the goings-on here, and that's Yahweh Himself. Sure, Yahweh begins chapter 8 with a vague command to take the city and set a trap, but past that, what is recorded here are choices Joshua made. God doesn't direct him to kill everyone and humiliate the king. God doesn't rebuke it either, but often the vilest moments in Scripture aren't at the hands of God, but the hands of men. God is suspiciously absent for a long time in this passage, and it leads me to conclude that this passage is meant to be taken as a description of what happened in the aftermath. The problem is that we often take passages like these and make them prescriptions for who God is or how we are to act. Big shocker here, not everything in Scripture is supposed to be emulated, and often when God is absent from a story, it says more about us than it does Him.

Is Marcion right to see Jesus and Yahweh as opposing forces? No, not when a contextual evaluation of these writings is viewed within their culture. To make matters worse for him, Marcion had to cut out a plethora of Scriptures to validate his view, and I'm afraid, dear Dante, so will you.

Dante's Rebuttal: God is Not the Only God
There is a lot of bloodshed in the Old Testament.
Thank you for making that point for me.
There are also Levitical laws about slaves that
are hard to digest as just. There are stories of
curses. There's the *Sophie's Choice* that God gives
David as retribution: pestilence, famine, or
war (2 Samuel 24). You take one book, Joshua,
and try to denigrate a reading of the OT that
winces at God's behavior. That's rich!

I'm not saying this to be merely adversarial.
It's difficult to reconcile righteous Yahweh
with Jesus, who calls God to forgive his
murderers while they are torturing him. I
think an honest read creates whiplash. Is it
not fair to at least acknowledge that?

But alright, you allege I'm picking and choosing…

let's go to the bedrock of the Torah: the 10 Commandments. Starting with numero uno:

> *You shall have no other gods before me.*
> Exodus 20:3 ESV

Sure makes it sound like he's one of many, no?

Go to the 2nd commandment. Perhaps that'll clear it up.

> *You shall not make for yourself a carved image,*
> *or any likeness of anything that is in heaven above,*
> *or that is in the earth beneath, or that*
> *is in the water under the earth.*
> *You shall not bow down to them or serve them,*
> *for I the Lord your God am a jealous God…*
> Exodus 20:4-5 ESV

If Yahweh is one of many, how do we know he's the right one?

Chris's Rebuttal: An Honest Reading Of Scripture is Possible

I agree. An honest reading of Scripture certainly can leave one with whiplash. It feels all over the place. That's why it's so important we don't interpret Scripture through our Western lens. We have to, best as we can, learn and understand the culture the book was composed in and written to, all while not allowing our own biases into the mix.

I think both of us have made a pretty clear case

throughout this work that there are other "gods", no? That Yahweh exists alongside other spiritual beings is almost certainly a given, whether we are talking about the Prince of Rome, Chemosh, Azazel, or Santa Muerte.

The key, though, is that these "gods" aren't worthy of the title. They're imposters to the one true Lord, whether you agree with His methods or not. At least, that's what an honest reading of Scripture tells you.

Dante's Rebuttal: How do You Know Who's the Imposter?

"Yahweh exists alongside other spiritual beings." ← You said that.

If Yahweh is one of many, how do we know he's the best? Before you answer that, I assume you'd point me back to the life, work, death, and resurrection of Jesus from Galilee. Great comeback! But my shipbuilder, who you rightly identified as a dude named Marcion, doesn't think that the God that Jesus calls his Father... is Yahweh.

Let's talk Plato!

The broad-shouldered philosopher, some 400 years before Jesus breaks stuff in Jerusalem's temple, imagined what he called a "demiurge". In the Socratic dialogue *Timaeus*, Plato conceives of the demiurge as a creationist artisan. This demiurge is the craftsman of the cosmos; the sculptor of the physical world. The demiurge, however, is distinct from the highest God (often referred to in Platonic circles as the "monad"). In Plato's cosmology, the highest God has a thought, and that thought is the demiurge. The demiurge then creates the world.

Our boy Marcion comes along and links the demiurge to Yahweh. Now, Marcion gets a bad rap from some of the early church's heresy hunters as rendering Yahweh as a villain. That's not really the case. Rather than some early version of Batman's Joker, an agent of chaos for chaos' sake, Marcion saw Yahweh as a god obsessed with justice. He created the world, and he wants his world to function well. He wants it to be a good world. So the creator god is interacting with humanity, creating the flood that nearly wiped out all of humanity, and then, as seen in the 10 Commandments and Levitical laws, zealously holding his people to a strict moral code.

For Marcion, and even moreso, a group of folks called the Gnostics, Jesus came to earth to point humanity not towards this craftsman demiurge, but to the God above him. While Marcion sees Yahweh as a righteous god, that unmitigating zeal for complete righteousness is at odds with the Gospel and its focus on grace and love. Adolf Harnacki, in his "History of Dogma", writes of Marcion:

"The law which rules nature and man appeared to [Marcion] to accord with the characteristics of this god and the kind of law revealed by him, and therefore it seemed credible to him that this god is the creator and lord of the world... Marcion placed the good God of love in opposition to the creator of the world. This God has only been revealed in Christ."

Note that Marcion's Yahweh is the "lord of the world". Match that to this statement the Apostle Paul makes in his 2nd letter to the Corinthians:

In their case the god of this world has blinded
the minds of the unbelievers,
to keep them from seeing the light of the gospel
of the glory of Christ,
who is the image of God.
2 Corinthians 4:4 ESV

Check it out: according to both Paul and Marcion, the "god of this world" is keeping folks from seeing the truth. Sounds pretty Satanic, no?

Chris's Rebuttal: The Totality Of Scripture Directly Contradicts The Gnostics

It's certainly an interesting hypothesis, and I'll admit ol' Marci did his homework. However, there is still one big glaring flaw within your logic.

First, let's talk about those Gnostics you mentioned. Gnosticism is a belief system that has almost always been the ugly step-brother of Christianity. Nobody's quite sure when it got started. Still, the movement came into complete formation around the second century CE. Gnosticism, or at least a proto-version of their beliefs, seems to exist alongside the appearance of the early church. Many commentators believe some of Paul's letters, like Galatians, were written to combat these emerging ideas.

*I'm amazed that you are so quickly deserting the one
who called you by the grace of Christ
to follow another gospel.
It's not really another gospel, but certain
people are confusing you,
and they want to change the gospel of Christ.
However, even if we ourselves or a heavenly angel
should ever preach anything different
from what we preached to you,
they should be under a curse. I'm
repeating what we've said before:
if anyone preaches something different
from what you received,
they should be under a curse!*
Galatians 1:6-9 CEB

Those are strong words from Paul. This false teaching was so dangerous that it required his rebuke twice in the same passage! So, what exactly did these Gnostics believe?

As you stated, the Gnostics liked Plato's idea of

the demiurge god vs. the monad god. One Creator against one All-Powerful. They borrowed these ideas from Plato and used Jewish and Christian texts to justify their beliefs that Yahweh was against the one true God who sent Christ. Then they pushed those ideas even further. They saw what the demiurge created as wholly evil. This "god of justice" tainted the entire material world, and he locked divine elements within the human meat cages he made. It's here where Jesus comes in as a complete spiritual being to point the fallen material world back to the divine. Only through the "divine" knowledge that Jesus brings can the spiritual elements locked within our human meat cages be freed to return to the monad.

Does this ring any bells yet? Demiurge vs. monad. Material vs. spiritual. Knowledge vs. flesh. Good vs. evil. The whole thing reeks of dualism.

You remember dualism: the idea that there are two distinct and opposing parts? In our case, gnosticism is just dualism hiding under a bad Scooby Doo mask.

It's easy to see how people like Marcion and the Gnostics could get a dualistic impression from certain Scriptures. Remember, though, that big glaring logical flaw I mentioned? Even a cursory reading of Scripture makes it pretty hard to pit Yahweh against Jesus, and to overcome that flaw, both Marcion and the Gnostics had to heavily redact and all together throw out A LOT of Scripture.

Marcion and later Gnostics threw out Matthew, Mark, and John, and only kept very certain parts of Luke's Gospel. Why? Because it couldn't fit within their dualistic belief system.

Consider just briefly the birth account of Jesus in Matthew. An angel appears to Joseph and tells him that his son will be the one written about by the prophet Isaiah. This directly connects Jesus to the God of the Old Testament. Or what of the 46 times in Matthew, Mark, and John that Jesus refers to himself as the "Son of Man", a title directly connecting him to the prophecies given by Yahweh himself? That's not even mentioning Paul's letters Marcion threw out, that directly quote from the same prophecies. What about the first two chapters in Luke, which Marcion and the gnostics completely cut out because Jesus' genealogy directly links Him to the God who created Adam? Or how about the forbidden chapter of Isaiah 53, a passage so deeply pointing to Jesus as the Messiah that even Jewish rabbis refuse to read it?

Really though, it's the book of John that is Marcion's worst nightmare. The Gospel begins so terribly for him.

In the beginning was the Word
and the Word was with God and the Word was God.
The Word was with God in the beginning.

*Everything came into being through the Word,
and without the Word, nothing came into being.
What came into being through the Word was life,
and the life was the light for all people.*
John 1:1-4 CEB

John explicitly links Jesus, the Word, as the same God who created everything back in Genesis. No mention of a higher god. Heck, John says that the Word "created" everything. If anything, that makes Jesus the demiurge!

It just gets worse from there, though. John goes on to record 7 "I Am" statements made by Jesus. Why would this matter? Because this language is intentional. In Exodus 3, we see Yahweh, the God of Israel, talking to Moses in a burning bush. Then, we get this exchange:

*But Moses said to God, "If I now come to
the Israelites and say to them,
"the God of your ancestors has sent me
to you, they are going to ask me,
'What's this God's name?' What am
I supposed to say to them?"
God said to Moses, "I Am Who I Am.
So say to the Israelites, 'I Am has sent me to you'"*
Exodus 3:13-14 CEB

Do you get it? Jesus is the same I Am that sent Moses to the people of Israel. You simply cannot separate Yahweh and Jesus into two separate and opposing entities without changing the Scriptures wildly.

Dante's Rebuttal: Four Things

I have some thoughts:

1. Demiurge sounds a lot like demogorgon. *Stranger Things* is the best!

2. "Human meat cages": name of your next metal band!

3. I want to start a Gnostic church called "The Gnu Gnostics" and our symbol would be the wildebeests that trampled Mufasa to death.

4. Do you know the difference between Satanists and Luciferians?

What do you have to say to that?!

Chris's Rebuttal: Four Things, Back at Ya!

1. *Stranger Things* is the best!

2. Only if you agree to write all the lyrics and scream!

3. That's perfect; change nothing about it. NO NOTES!

4. I believe Satanists worship Satan in the traditional sense. Whereas Luciferians think Satan got a bad rap and is the true God, whereas Yahweh is evil. Correct?

Dante's Rebuttal: Let's at Least Hear those Gnu Gnostics Out

The name Lucifer is the Latinized version of the phrase "morning star". The name is generally associated with Satan because it shows up in that ominous Isaiah 14 passage that we've recounted more than once thus far, wherein it appears Isaiah is recounting an angelic fall from grace.

> *How you've fallen from heaven,*
> *morning star, son of dawn!*
> *You are cut down to earth,*
> *helpless on your back!*
> Isaiah 14:12 CEB

This Lucifer, the 'morning star', fell from heaven. Historically, folks have associated the 'morning star' in the sky with Venus. Besides the moon and the sun, Venus is the most consistently bright light bulb up in the sky, and the one that is still glowing and viewable in the early morning. We could easily run off course here and talk about Venus, femininity, and Satan, but we already covered some of that ground in our Lilith debate, so I'll do my best to stay the course. Let's boil it down to this: the morning star is the brightest star.

Now check this out: right at the end of the Bible, five verses from the very end of the whole big shebang, the morning star shows up again.

> *I, Jesus, have sent my angel to bear witness*
> *to all of you about these things for the churches.*
> *I'm the root and descendant of David,*
> *the bright morning star.*
> Revelation 22:16 CEB

What am I trying to say, that Jesus is Satan? No. No, I'm not.

Your main argument appears to be that Gnostics don't use all of Scripture. I'll sum up my rebuttal succinctly:

1. No one uses all of Scripture. Women don't cover their heads in church anymore, even though Paul commands it (1 Corinthians 1:15). Similarly, in Acts, when the early church is figuring out what makes a Christian a Christian, their big requirements are to stay sexually pure and not eat animals that have been strangled or eat blood. We don't exactly include anti-strangulation of animals in our Christian creeds. I live in the Texas Bible belt: folks love Jesus and love their steaks still gushing with blood.

2. The Gnostics, just like the early Christians, had various sects. As you pointed out, some sects had a more rigid corpus of holy books, while others borrowed more liberally from New Testament literature. Both John and Paul are revered by a bundle of Gnostics, including a dude (Gnu?) named Valentinus, who is probably the most famous Gnostic.

3. From a protestant Christian's perspective: yeah, the Gnostics were picking and choosing. But when you look with eyes outside of the mainstream, you can make the same case about Protestants. They didn't like the concept of

purgatory, so they didn't include the Apocrypha in the Bible. They didn't like the Gnostic-ness of the Gospel of Thomas, so they buried it, despite its early dating. Same goes with the Shepherd of Hermes and perhaps Clement's epistles as well. Marcion lived in the 2nd century, around 200 years before the Christian canon was formalized, so claiming that he was picking and choosing is a bit premature, no?

4. Most scholars agree that John 8 was pushed into the Gospel at some later point. Our earliest manuscripts don't include that chapter. Same goes with the end of Mark (which is remarkable considering how much theological weight we put on the resurrection). Sooooooo… aren't mainline early Christians guilty of not only picking and choosing, but also adding? How is this different from what the Gnostics did?

I brought the Lucifer thing up (oh, and by-the-by, Luciferians see themselves as distinct from Satanists in that Satanists worship carnality, whereas Luciferians are much more like Gnostics, wanting to ascend beyond the body to become beings of light… perhaps morning light) to point out that our Bible is vast. It contains myriad voices with myriad ideas. Saying that one needs to read and exegete the whole of the Bible in order to properly apply any portion of it seems like a Herculean task. But, in case I haven't made my point strong enough that there is more than an ounce of Gnostickiness in the New Testament, let's take a look at a few more examples:

> *For those who live according to the flesh*
> *set their minds on the things of the flesh,*
> *but those who live according to the Spirit*
> *set their minds on the things of the Spirit.*
> *For to set the mind on the flesh is death,*
> *but to set the mind on the Spirit is life and peace.*
> *For the mind that is set on the flesh is hostile to God,*
> *for it does not submit to God's law; indeed, it cannot.*
> *Those who are in the flesh cannot please God.*
> *You, however, are not in the flesh but in the Spirit,*
> *if in fact the Spirit of God dwells in you.*
> *Anyone who does not have the Spirit of*
> *Christ does not belong to him.*
> Romans 8:5-10 ESV

Here, in the midst of one of the hallmark passages in all the Bible, Paul makes a couple very Gnostic points. Gnostics saw the physical world as evil and spirit as good. Salvation comes from the soul's escape from the physical world. Secondly, several Gnostic sects divided humanity into three groups: the elect, the half-elect (for lack of a better word), and the animalistic humans. Some humans were merely carnal for those Gnostics, with no hint of the eternal divine in them, while the chosen elect were not children of the physical world, but children of the light. It's not hard to interpret Paul's passage in this light.

*If with Christ you died to the elemental
spirits of the world,
why, as if you were still alive in the world,
do you submit to regulations—"Do not
handle, Do not taste, Do not touch"
(referring to things that all perish as they are used)—
according to human precepts and teachings?
These have indeed an appearance
of wisdom in promoting
self-made religion and asceticism
and severity to the body,
but they are of no value in stopping
the indulgence of the flesh.*
Colossians 2:20-23 ESV

Gnosticism has a complex mythology with higher and lower heavenly spirits. Elemental spirits sound like a low class of divinity. Paul rails here against physical laws; perhaps like eating strangled animals and feasting on animal blood? Did the Jerusalem Council have it wrong?

At the very center of Gnosticism is the concept of secret or privileged revelation. Paul's not afraid to bring in his own inaccessible, unverifiable mystery nuggets:

*I must go on boasting.
Though there is nothing to be gained by it,
I will go on to visions and revelations of the Lord.
I know a man in Christ who fourteen years
ago was caught up to the third heaven*

> *—whether in the body or out of the*
> *body I do not know, God knows.*
> *And I know that this man was*
> *caught up into paradise—*
> *whether in the body or out of the body*
> *I do not know, God knows—*
> *and he heard things that cannot be*
> *told, which man may not utter.*
> 2 Corinthians 12:1-4 ESV

Pretty secret stuff. Not only secrety stuff, but also leveled! Paul references visiting the third heaven! How many levels of heaven are there? Gnostics are very interested in a hierarchical view of the heavens which contain many tiers. This statement fits right along with Gnostic orthodoxy.

I shall go on.

As we've already shared, the roots of Gnosticism are very much Platonic. Plato's demiurge, aka craftsman, is the maker of the physical world, sure, but the cave analogy lets us in on the secret: stuff ain't what it seems to be. According to Plato, the demiurge has just made copies of the eternal, spiritual world.

Referencing the Old Testament and the temple and priests, the writer of Hebrews states:

> *They serve a copy and shadow of*
> *the heavenly things…*
> Hebrews 8:5a ESV

A chapter later, the writer continues to build his argument for why the new covenant and Christ's work on the cross supersedes the old covenant and laws:

> *Thus it was necessary for the copies*
> *of the heavenly things*
> *to be purified with these rites,*
> *but the heavenly things themselves with*
> *better sacrifices than these.*
> *For Christ has entered, not into holy*
> *places made with hands,*
> *which are copies of the true things...*
> Hebrews 9:23-24a ESV

Then,

> *For since the law has but a shadow*
> *of the good things to come*
> *instead of the true form of these realities...*
> Hebrews 10:1a ESV

This isn't merely lip service to Plato, this is full-on usurpation!

Let's pivot to the Gospels for a moment. Why was it necessary that Jesus be born to a virgin? Why was his DNA Daddy the Holy Spirit and not good ol' Joseph? Christian orthodoxy has informed us that this is because Jesus needed to be born without the sin nature that we continue to inherit from Adam. But our doctrine of original sin took centuries to calcify. In the second century, as the Gnostics were gaining footing, their rationale for Jesus' divine father made just as much theological sense as our present orthodoxy: Jesus is spirit, that's why he came to the earth with a spiritual nature, so as to show us that the way to salvation is by escaping the confines of the physical world.

Okay, alright... perhaps I've belabored the Gnostic virtues for too long. Why have I done so? I wanted to establish the historical roots to my argument. Calling the God of the Old Testament Satan, or at least a villain, is not a modern phenomenon. Before the New Testament was codified, voices from among scriptural readers were already struggling with this notion. Look at Hebrews one more time:

> *For if that first covenant had been faultless,*
> *there would have been no occasion*
> *to look for a second.*
> Hebrews 8:7 ESV

Who created that first covenant? Isn't the Bible affirming that God created a faulty covenant?
If this God of the Old Testament made the first covenant faulty (read: imperfect), then there are only two options. One, he made a mistake. Or. Two, he purposefully made something broken.

> *And the LORD was sorry that he had*
> *made man on the earth,*
> *and it grieved him to his heart. So the LORD said,*
> *"I will blot out man whom I have created*

> *from the face of the land,*
> *man and animals and creeping things*
> *and birds of the heavens,*
> *for I am sorry that I have made them."*
> Genesis 6:6-7 ESV

Contrast that to the words of Jesus.

> *The thief comes only to steal and kill and destroy.*
> *I came that they may have life and*
> *have it abundantly.*
> John 10:10 ESV

One drowns the world, one saves the world.

Chris' Conclusion: Satan Cannot Be God

There is an old parable among pastors that may help us see a little bit clearer. One day, Satan and a high-ranking demon are walking along a well-traveled path and conversing. They stumble upon a man who has just picked up a shiny and beautiful piece of truth about God off the ground. The demon shrieks, "Master! Whatever will we do?!?! This man has just found a truth about God; surely it will be impossible to deceive him now!"

The old devil laughs slyly to himself, "Fear not, for we will convince the man that it is the only truth about God, and he will build a religion out of only it."

This is the same trap Marcion, the Gnostics, and the Luciferians have fallen into.

First off, to your point that everyone does some picking and choosing in regards to Scripture... Well, yeah, no duh. Isn't that kind of the point of religion in the first place; one group picking and choosing what they believe to be holy and inspired against what they do not?

The problem is if we start disqualifying everything based on people picking and choosing their authoritative texts, we are going to find that it's turtles all the way down. But just because everyone does, it doesn't mean everyone does it equally.

"Whataboutisms" is problematic because it's easy to point at anyone, say the protestants, and say, "well, what about them denying the Apocrypha?" What they often fail to illustrate are the disparities in methodologies between two groups. You rightfully noted that Marcion is several hundred years ahead of the first official canonization of books from the church. Why is that? Well, one good reason is that Marcion was one dude, but the church was composed of many dudes (and don't even @ me about not including women in this description, in the words of Chance the Rapper, "*Good Burger* shoulda taught ya we all dudes").

Marcion didn't have anyone to push back against his canon, or at least he didn't listen to them when they did. In contrast, the church had several hundred years of debates across a broad group of perspectives and beliefs. The most significant difference is the value of the generational community against an almost entirely solo effort. Marcion may have found a piece of the truth about God being good, but without the wider community, he built a religion wholly hung on his understanding.

What about the Gnostics, though? They were a larger community than just one man. They, however, have their problems. You know better than most that, save the *Gospel of Thomas*, all Gnostic texts date impossibly late to have been written by their alleged authors. Categorically, these texts are far later than their New Testament counterparts. But what about those New Testament parts that sound Gnostic?

Sure, snag some verses from Paul out of context, and he sounds pretty Gnostic. Then again, snag some other verses, and Paul sounds like the most anti-Gnostic MF'er you've ever meant.

> *See to it that nobody enslaves you with*
> *philosophy and foolish deception,*
> *which conform to human traditions*
> *and the way the world thinks and*
> *acts rather than Christ.*
> Colossians 2:8 CEB

> *Now concerning meat that has been*
> *sacrificed to a false god:*
> *We know that we all have knowledge.*

> *Knowledge makes people arrogant,*
> *but love builds people up.*
> *If anyone thinks they know something,*
> *they don't yet know as much as they should know.*
> *But if someone loves God, then*
> *they are known by God.*
> 1st Corinthians 8:1-3 CEB

What are we to do!?!? Throw up our hands and say, "There's no hope in understanding Scripture?" Is it really too herculean a task? Are we entirely without hope?

Of course not! Is there a lot of Scripture to understand? For sure! But it's not a lost cause. This is where Christian discipleship comes into play. We are surrounded by a vast community of those who have come before us throughout Christianity's two millennia! If Newton stood on the shoulders of giants, we stand humbly on the shoulders of millions! Those millions reveal an important truth that the Gnostics have overlooked: God cares for the physical and spiritual.

Does God drown the whole creation in a fever dream of rebooting it into an intangible spiritual paradise? No! He preserves Noah and his family and the world's creatures so that the physical can continue. Does Yahweh, creator of the universe, abandon his creation without hope? No! He walks with them in a garden. He goes before them in a cloud of fire to protect them. He gives them a law to live by. Is that law perfect? Well, only as perfect as it can be in the hands of finite creations. Thus, the need for an infinite being arose, and since Yahweh is the only one capable of fulfilling that role, He Himself came down to live in the flesh and blood and muck and mud with His creation.

To the dismay of Gnostics, Jesus is literally God in meat form. He sleeps, weeps, laughs, and eats! Is there anything more human than eating? Then, as if to prove His total meatiness, He dies for His creation. And when He defeats death, does He do it in some spiritual ghost form? No! He resurrects in full-body, so much so that Thomas doesn't believe until he can feel the nail-pierced wrists!

Is God spirit? Yes, the Gnostics got that truth right, but they failed to build their religion around a God who is as much spirit as He is flesh. If meat-god Jesus didn't care about the physical, then why would He say:

> *Aren't two sparrows sold for a small coin?*
> *But not one of them will fall to the ground*
> *without your Father knowing about it already.*
> *Even the hairs of your head are all counted.*
> *Don't be afraid.*
> *You are worth more than many sparrows.*
> Matthew 10:29-31 CEB

Yahweh cares for the physical well-being of a worthless bird like the sparrow, and we too can be confident He cares for our physical needs as well as our spiritual. We don't need to exegete every verse to see this narrative spread across every corner of Scripture. This thread runs from the beginning when Yahweh calls His creation "good" through the end. In Revelation, after Jesus has defeated death and our good pal Satan, we get this scene:

> *Then I saw a new heaven and a new earth,*
> *for the former heaven and the former*
> *earth had passed away,*
> *and the sea was no more.*
> *I saw the holy city, New Jerusalem, coming*
> *down out of heaven from God,*
> *made ready as a bride beautifully*
> *dressed for her husband.*
> *I heard a loud voice from the throne say,*
> *"Look! God's dwelling is here with humankind.*
> *He will dwell with them, and they will be his peoples.*
> *God himself will be with them as their God.*
> *He will wipe away every tear from their eyes.*
> *Death will be no more.*
> *There will be no mourning, crying, or pain anymore,*
> *for the former things have passed away."*
> *Then the one seated on the throne said,*
> *"Look! I'm making all things new.'*
> Revelation 21:1-5 CEB

Yahweh recreates the heavens AND THE EARTH! The physical world as well as the spiritual! He proclaims over His victory that He is making "all things" new again! Not just the spiritual but the totality of all of creation is remade to live with Him on earth in the New Jerusalem. Does the Gnostic demiurge do that? Does monad? Nope! Only Yahweh can!

But enough about God, let's talk about Satan. Could Satan be the good guy all along? Well, you said it yourself earlier. "*What am I trying to say? --that Jesus is Satan? No. I'm not.*" Whew, thanks for that. As we already established, Jesus is Yahweh in meat form. So you do the math.

But I know you too well; you aren't content with such a simple answer. Rather than dredge up the arguments, we've both already made, let's go somewhere new. Somewhere many folks go but should be far more fearful to—the book of Job.

I don't want to spend too much time on the setup here because I think this book is one of the best known. Instead, I'll let one of my all-time favorite metal songs from Tourniquet give us a quick summary.

> "Satan called upon the Lord
> 'I must perform a test
> To prove that faith in God
> Is contingent on being blessed'
> One of the richest men of the second millennium
> Job was stripped of all his wealth
> Three daughters and seven sons
> He tore his robe

> And shaved his head
> Fell to the ground, worshipped God and said:
> I was naked when I came here
> I'll be naked when I leave here
> The Lord gave it
> So He can take it
> All away"

Okay, that's a pretty great intro to the beginning of the book. As it goes on, Satan comes to God a second time and asks to attack Job's faith again, only to have a very similar result. Then poof! Suddenly, Satan leaves. The rest of this terribly long book is a dialogue between Job, his awful friends, and God. Ultimately, Job learns to praise God even when nothing goes his way.

I know the first thing you're going to point out, so save your breath. The name given to Satan here is the Hebrew word *"hassatan"* and is best translated as "the opposer" or "the adversary". Because Hebrew is a fun language, we can't be sure if words are proper names or titles or adjectives because of the lack of capitalization. We (and by "we" I mean the good people who do the hard work of translating ancient languages for us) have to infer from context if something is a proper name or not.

So the argument goes, "How do we know Satan is really who Christian tradition says he is if we can't figure out what's an adjective and what's a name?"

That's a great question. Unfortunately, it doesn't

have any satisfying answers. As we've explored so far, Satan has a long and complicated history. To frustrate matters even further, we don't know if Job is a true story or an allegory. If it is a true story, there's almost no way to date it. Still, it certainly seems like much of our ideas about the devil come from the first two chapters.

I'm devolving a bit here because this is where our Satan story begins to unravel. What is essential for this argument, though, is this: even though we don't know the true meaning of the phrase *"hasśatan"* there are a couple of important things to take from the book of Job.

1. This story was held dearly by the ancient Jews as early as the 6th century BCE.
2. The book of Job has a celestial being who seems to act against the wishes of God.
3. This being eventually came to be known in Christian circles as Satan, later named by Jesus and the writers of the New Testament.

While there is a lot we don't know here, we can see one truth the Luciferians get right; there is some celestial being with his own agenda. What they miss, however, is that this being cannot be Yahweh or Jesus. The Scriptures are clear about Jesus and Yahweh's relation to each other. Satan is portrayed as someone other than God. Who is he? We will get there, but for now, this truth stands above all else; Satan is not God. Perhaps the final words of the Tourniquet song I quoted earlier pack a bitter punch for us:

> "He who puts the Lord on trial
> Puts himself on the stand"

CHAPTER XIII

Who is Satan?

Dante's Conclusion

I told you there was a monster at the end of this book. Maybe you didn't believe me.

There's a relevant question we've yet to contend with: why is the Old Testament so bereft of Satan and demons? When Jesus comes to Israel, demons are abundant. There's something like 5,000 demons within one fella that Jesus exorcizes. There's no Satan tempting Abraham or Moses or Isaiah. He only comes to Jesus. To go even further, anything about the afterlife at all is a stretch in the Old Testament. Why?

Perhaps we can't answer that question. The question we *can* begin to answer is...

When?

When did the afterlife, demons, a final judgment day, and heaven and hell begin to manifest themselves in the Jewish zeitgeist? We see these things clearly begin to take form in the post-exilic, intertestamental time period. There's a treasure trove of apocryphal writings during this age that break fresh ground on these topics, some of which we've already encountered (such as the book of Enoch). So then, Jesus didn't himself introduce these ideas to the world. They had already been circulating throughout Israel for centuries before his incarnation.

As Christians, we've come to accept, either explicitly or implicitly, that God reveals Himself to us in time and in a progressive manner. Abraham knew only that God would bless the nations through his offspring, not that God would incarnate himself as one of Abe's descendants.

So how has God revealed Satan and his ilk to us?

I'd like to propose a theory. We're at the endgame now, the final pages of this book. Perhaps it's wrong to introduce a new concept. In debate class they told me it was anathema to introduce something new in your closing arguments. Well, I guess you can anathematize me now. Here we are, ready to meet the monster at the end of this book. Take a big breath. This'll be a bumpy ride.

Let's start with the Hindus.

Hinduism has an extensive corpus of sacred writings. The oldest of their texts are four volumes called the *Vedas*. Dating them is a bit sketchy, but historians are confident that the *Rig Veda* is the oldest. Scholars generally date its conception to somewhere around 1200 BCE. The first word in the *Rig Veda*, a text that may predate any Biblical text, is "*Agni.*" Agni is both a god, and the word for fire.

Agni.

A translation of the opening lines of the *Rig Veda*, as described by wikisource, reads:

> *1. I, Laud Agni, the chosen Priest, God, minister of sacrifice,*
> *The hotar, lavishest of wealth.*
> *2. Worthy is Agni to be praised by living as by ancient seers.*
> *He shall bring hitherward the Gods."*

Agni will bring the other gods.

Fascinatingly, the prime gods of the *Vedas*, such as Agni (as well as Indra and others), aren't very popular in Hinduism anymore. Those old gods have been supplanted by others. A brief purview of Agni's Wikipedia page tells us that, "Agni is originally conceptualized as the ultimate source of the *creator-maintainer-destroyer* triad, then one of the trinities, as the one who ruled the earth." Agni, in the Vedic mind, is a foundational thought that leads to creation and destruction. But, uh, we're getting ahead of ourselves. That's enough Hinduism for now.

Let's migrate to another religion.

There's this guy. Maybe you've heard of him. He generally is known by the name Zoroaster. Some folks call him Zarathustra. When he was thirty years old, hanging out in a river in either modern day Iran, Tajikistan, or Afghanistan, God appeared to him. Or so he says. God showed Zoroaster how to live rightly. So Zoroaster lived rightly. He attracted some followers, and badabing-badaboom, you've got yourself a religion.

There is much that can be said about Zoroastrianism (gotta work on Fun w/ Zoroastrianism someday). We'll start here: Zoroastrian custom and ritual is based around an eternal flame: aka *Agni*. Almost all of their rituals have some aspect of sacrificial burnings and whatnot. For Zoroaster, Agni (or Atar in his native Avestan tongue) is God's "light of revelation." Fire is, in and of itself, both kind of a thing and kind of not a thing. You can't grasp it. You can't hold it like you can hold my hand. And yet, fire is obviously a real thing, giving us light and illuminating everything around it. Zoroastrians don't worship agni/flame. They don't comprehend fire as a god, but rather, as a metaphor or instrument by which we can begin to comprehend God.

When did Zoroaster live? The speculation is all over the place on that one. Some say 600 BCE, others as early as 1200 BCE. If it's the latter, that would line up closely with the writing of the *Rig*

Veda. Coincidence?

Zoroastrianism came to become the dominant religion of the Persian empire. Zoroastrianism itself is fascinating, because it appears to have gone from a monotheistic religion to a dualistic one, to later having a complete polytheistic pantheon. That goes against the religious evolution flow that many historians propose (going from shamanism → polytheism → henotheism → monotheism → atheism), but whatever. Zoroastrians dance to their own tantric beat.

We'd likely have nothing to say about Zoroastrians had it not been for a special little fella coming to power. We know him as Cyrus the Great. Cyrus takes the Persians from being a semi-nomadic, nothingburger people, to conquering more land than anyone before him in human history. Cyrus deserves a seat next to Alexander the Great and Genghis Khan in the conquerors' hall of fame.

It goes like this. Cyrus conquers Babylon. Turns out, that's where Daniel, Shadrach, Meshach, and Abednego all were hanging out in bondage. The Jewish people had been captive there for some time. Cyrus comes in and lets the Jewish people return home. Once there, they ask him if they can rebuild their temple to their god Yahweh. Cyrus grants them this wish. Multiple accounts in the Jewish Bible overflow with adoration for the foreign king. Ezra and 2 Chronicles both share this account:

> *Now in the first year of Cyrus king of Persia,*
> *that the word of the Lord by the mouth*
> *of Jeremiah might be fulfilled,*
> *the Lord stirred up the spirit of Cyrus king of Persia,*
> *so that he made a proclamation throughout*
> *all his kingdom and also put it in writing:*
> *"Thus says Cyrus king of Persia, 'The*
> *LORD, the God of heaven,*
> *has given me all the kingdoms of the earth,*
> *and he has charged me to build him a house*
> *at Jerusalem, which is in Judah.*
> *Whoever is among you of all his people,*
> *may the Lord his God be with him.*
> *Let him go up'"*
> 2 Chronicles 36:22-23 ESV

Notice that the Chronicler (and Ezra) has Cyrus not just allowing the Jews to worship their own God, but explicitly calling God Yahweh (The LORD), God of heaven. Cyrus even declares that this God of the Hebrews has given the nations over to him. In this passage, it appears that Cyrus is actively serving the God of the Jews.

Was Cyrus the Great of Persia a God follower?

Non-Biblical sources testify that Cyrus did indeed allow the Jews to return to their homeland and worship Yahweh. One such source, however, a cylinder called the Cyrus Cylinder, has Cyrus stating that he also allowed the Babylonians to worship Marduk, "the great lord". Generally speaking, Marduk and Yahweh are not friends... Cyrus' fidelity to Yahweh might not be exactly universal.

A passage in Isaiah really lays it all on the table for us. It begins:

> *Thus says the Lord to his anointed, to Cyrus,*
> *whose right hand I have grasped...*
> Isaiah 45:1a ESV

Cyrus is God's anointed. Who else is anointed by God? The Old Testament offers us Kings Saul, David, and Solomon as anointed by God at various times. Perhaps we don't need to read into it any more than that. God anoints kings. Cyrus shares that distinction with Israel's kings, so perhaps that's that. But there are a couple other usages of anointing that Scripture offers us.

> *He allowed no one to oppress them;*
> *for their sake he rebuked kings:*
> *"Do not touch my anointed ones;*
> *do my prophets no harm."*
> 1 Chronicles 16:21-22 ESV

The text here refers to God's chosen people. They are his anointed ones. Then there's one other fella who gets the title of "anointed one" in Daniel 9:25-26. That passage is fraught with ambiguity, and Christian commentators have been battling over it for generations, but suffice it to say, this other anointed one seems likely to be Jesus himself. Anywho... Cyrus is in good company.

Anyway you slice it, Cyrus and Yahweh appeared to have a good relationship. But being friendly is one thing... who did Cyrus actually worship?

Although we don't have direct quotes from Cyrus himself, his predecessors and successors all worshiped the God of Zoroaster: Ahura Mazda. In *A History of Zoroastrianism: Volume II*, historian Mary Boyce writes that there is "good evidence that the Persian king (Cyrus) was not only a believer (in Zoroastrianism), but one committed to establishing the faith throughout his realms...." (p. 46).

Cyrus the Great worshiped Ahura Mazda, and his people introduced Zoroastrianism to the conquered world.

From the available evidence, we can conclude that Cyrus did not worship Yahweh, but his own dude, Ahura Mazda. Let's now circle back to that Isaiah passage for a bit. Yahweh is speaking directly to Cyrus here. What does God have to say to this non-Jewish king whom He's chosen to anoint?

> *Thus says the Lord to his anointed, to Cyrus,*
> *whose right hand I have grasped,*
> *to subdue nations before him*
> *and to loose the belts of kings,*

> *to open doors before him*
> *that gates may not be closed:*
> *"I will go before you*
> *and level the exalted places,*
> *I will break in pieces the doors of bronze*
> *and cut through the bars of iron,*
> *I will give you the treasures of darkness*
> *and the hoards in secret places,*
> *that you may know that it is I, the Lord,*
> *the God of Israel, who call you by your name.*
> Isaiah 45:1-3 ESV

God is talking to Cyrus, right? And here he's telling Cyrus that he'll give him victory in battle. These victories, so says God, will lead Cyrus to know that Yahweh, God of Israel, is the King over all.

The text gets even more intriguing...

> *For the sake of my servant Jacob,*
> *and Israel my chosen,*
> *I call you by your name,*
> *I name you, though you do not know me.*
> *I am the Lord, and there is no other,*
> *besides me there is no God;*
> *I equip you, though you do not know me,*
> *that people may know, from the rising of the sun*
> *and from the west, that there is none besides me;*
> *I am the Lord, and there is no other.*
> Isaiah 45:4-6 ESV

God is blessing Cyrus, though Cyrus does "not know me". What an odd passage? I can't think of any other Biblical passage that is quite like it. There are, of course, numerous passages wherein God uses foreign rulers to accomplish his will. That happens all the time. But the relationship here sounds different. It sounds intimate. To my ears, it sounds as if Yahweh is inviting Cyrus into a relationship with him.

The passage goes on in Isaiah 45, with God establishing his authority and dominion over all the earth.

> *I form light and create darkness;*
> *I make well-being and create calamity;*
> *I am the Lord, who does all these things.*
> Isaiah 45:6

Yahweh asserts himself as the creator of all things; both light and dark, good and bad. Potentially, this could be Yahweh answering the questions of Zoroastrians. But we'll touch on that later.

This little section of Isaiah ends with God's decree upon Cyrus:

> *I have stirred him up in righteousness,*
> *and I will make all his ways level;*
> *he shall build my city*
> *and set my exiles free,*
> *not for price or reward,"*
> *says the Lord of hosts.*
> Isaiah 45:13 ESV

Cyrus does set the Jews free. And he gives them

a commission to rebuild the temple. Cyrus clearly does the will of Yahweh.

Now we can spin our gaze back to asking, "why?". Why did God choose Cyrus? Was he just some random conqueror, or was there a particular purpose for his anointing?

Before the Jewish exile into Babylon, the Bible has almost nothing to say about any of these topics:
-The end of time
-Hell
-Demons
-Satan
-A Savior

It's only after the Jews come into contact with the Persians, and Persian Zoroastrianism, that we suddenly see this wellspring of ideas crop up in Jewish writings. We won't go into the intricacies of Zoroastrian doctrine, but a thirty-second overview is probably worth our time.

According to early Zoroastrianism:
There is one God, Ahura Mazda. He has good thoughts (Spenta Mainyu). These good thoughts are what create the world and everything in it. He also has something like an evil thought (Angra Mainyu). This evil thought is personified in the form of a big villain that later texts call Ahriman. Ahriman has sub-thoughts, and these guys populate the heavens as demonic beings (or perhaps just demonic thoughts). Likewise,

good sub-thoughts are personified as angels (and in later Zoroastrianism, gods themselves). Ahura Mazda is represented by light and associates only with the Spenta Mainyu (happy thoughts!).

In order to go to heaven, which is described as eternity in Ahura Mazda's presence, one must help the light defeat the darkness. Ahriman and his evil-thought kin are represented by the absence of light (or flame: *Agni*!). At the end of time, Ahura Mazda and those that follow him will defeat Ahriman in a final battle. After that, they'll be no more darkness. Death itself will be defeated. Much is written about in Zoroastrianism of this final climactic battle. Before the end, a savior will arise. This figure is called the "Saoshyant". This eschatological figure will renew all creation, make everything immortal, and lead the final battle to destroy all evil.

I'll let you make the connections to Christian theology yourself.

We started this journey by mentioning the connection that Zoroastrianism has with early Hinduism. Now we can perhaps see some overlap with Judaism and Christianity. Fascinatingly, perhaps there's even a parallel with Islam.

Zoroastrian texts state that after you die, you must walk across a bridge. On the other side of that bridge (the Chinvat bridge) is Ahura Mazda. Everyone longs to be in his presence. The bridge either appears as broad if you were a swell chap, or super-duper skinny if you weren't such a good person. If you fall off the bridge, congrats, you've punched your ticket into hell. In Islam, you must first walk across a bridge as narrow as a hair to get to paradise. Your sins weigh you down, deterring your progress. Are the similarities mere coincidence?

Speaking of hell, whether we like to admit it or not, our imagery of hell comes to us from Dante Alighieri's *The Divine Comedy*. In the epic poem, Virgil guides Dante in a vision through the many levels of hell. Then the twosome travel through purgatory. When Dante gets to heaven, his chauffeur changes. He is led onward by his long-lost love interest, Beatrice. Heaven is depicted as the planets and sun in our solar system, with God's presence finally being just beyond the cosmos. Pretty neat stuff. The funny thing is, while Dante wrote his epic poem in the 14th century, it sure seems like he stole his idea from a ninth-century Zoroastrian writer. In the *Book of Arda Viraf*, Arda is shown heaven and hell in a vision. His tour guide is a beautiful woman. The heavenlies are depicted as the moon, the sun, and the stars circling the prime center of heaven. He is then shown hell where demons are torturing folks in specific ways for their specific sins.

I belabor all this to show how subliminally impactful Zoroastrianism has been on almost all the major religions of the world.

Before moving back to our view of Satan, I'd like to force you to make a *Sophie's Choice*.

You can deny that Zoroastrianism had any substantive impact on how Christians and Jews view the angelic realm, Satan, and time's linearity. Choosing this option leaves us with a mystery left unsolved: why are demons so prevalent in 0 CE yet nowhere to be found in 1,000 BCE? Why does God not mention the Day of the Lord to Abraham, Isaac, or Jacob? Why doesn't God soothe Job by informing him of the existence of Heaven, where every wrong will be righted and justice flows down? These questions are left unanswered.

Our other option is to accept that Zoroastrianism introduced several metaphysical topics into our theology. However scary that sounds, it doesn't mean that we accept Zoroastrianism as non-heretical. It would simply mean that God revealed just enough to a man in a river in Iran, to bring about revelation to his people at the right time.

Don't believe me?

One more example.

Raphael, the painter, not the Ninja Turtle, is one of the most remarkable Renaissance painters that ever lived. His painting *The School of Athens* is particularly daunting, beautiful, and thought-provoking. The Vatican commissioned the painting, and it remains on display within the Vatican's walls to this day. It depicts a legion of philosophers. The prime figures, standing in the center, are, understandably, Plato and Aristotle. Seemingly everybody worth a darn in the Western world gets their likeness slapped onto this scene in the periphery. Not only that, but a bunch of folks get a tool or instrument to kind of show off what they were good at. Euclid gets a compass. Archimedes gets a chalkboard. And check it out! Our boy Zoroaster is here too! He holds a globe in his right hand (Remember Isaiah 45:1? *...whose right hand I have grasped to subdue nations before him..*). The globe isn't like one we'd see today. It has no continents or landmasses at all. Instead, it has stars. It's a map of stars.

Zoroastrians were big astrologists. Remember, these guys idealized light and flame (*Agni!*). Stars, being big balls of flame, were therefore pretty darn important. Zoroastrian priests were given the title: Magupati... or... Magi for short.

The wisemen who know to look for Jesus are "Magi from the East". What's East of Israel? Persia.

It seems overwhelmingly likely that the Magi were Zoroastrians. Now, the text doesn't say that the Magi were looking for a Savior (the Saoshyant), but why was it that they were so sure they needed to worship this baby? Perhaps their sacred texts prepared the way for them to hear God's direction.

Back to our *Sophie's Choice*. If you deny my Zoroastrian proposal, then you must end this Satanic hunt with no answers. Who is Satan? You don't know. The end.

You can come to that same conclusion even if you choose to believe that God has used Zoroastrianism to reveal himself. The lack of Satanic identity revealed in the Bible could very well still lead us to insist that this is a stone God doesn't care for us to turn over. We should focus on Jesus, set our eyes on Zion, and let the evil ones follow their own perdition.

HOWEVER!

If we all agree to hold this lightly, I'll suggest yet another path.

If it's through Zoroastrianism that we know about demons, then perhaps there's some truth we can mine from that tradition. We must be careful not to steer into heresy, but conform our minds to whatever is good, pure, and not in contradiction to what we know, through Jesus and his disciples to be true. That being said...

The problem with Satan (aside from his evilness), is that any sort of study on the fella tends to lead to dualism. The whole of history becomes a duel between God and Satan. Yet how could this be? Who is like God? No one. None. Nada. Zip. In many of our churches, we've fallen into this good vs. evil battle. In trying to seek good and not the world, we can fall into a cycle of giving Satan too much power.

Does Christianity propose a dualistic view of the world?

No.

It does not.

Perhaps Paul's words are reverberating in your mind as a rebuttal to my statement:

For we do not wrestle against flesh and blood,
but against the rulers, against the authorities,
against the cosmic powers over this present darkness,
against the spiritual forces of evil
in the heavenly places.
Ephesians 6:12 ESV

Notice the plurality here. There's a lot to battle against. It's not just one solitary Satan. It's a whole host of cosmic powers and darknesses and evils. Who are all these cats?

I form light and create darkness;
I make well-being and create calamity;
I am the Lord, who does all these things.
Isaiah 45:7 ESV

God is behind light and dark. He is the only creator. How can evil, ultimately, be placed on anyone's doorstep but Yahweh's?

Recall Augustine's syllogism:

> God created all things,
> All things God created are good,
> therefore, evil is not a thing.

This is a tough syllogism to get around. If you want evil to be a thing, then logically, you've got to either admit that God created something not good or that there's something out there that he didn't make.

Agni. Flame. To the ancient, it's a thing... and it's not a thing. What else could fit in that category?

A thought. Spenta Mainyu, or rather, an evil thought. Satan is an evil thought.

Dumb conclusion, right?

Recall what Jesus said when Peter got in his way?

Get behind me Satan!

Jesus calls Peter Satan.
Peter is Satan: the guy who Jesus said he'd give the keys to the kingdom.
That's Satan.

The word Satan, again, means adversary. When we look at sin, we tend to define it as anything that's against God. Satan, then, is any thought that is against God.

Can a fallen angel be Satan? Certainly. Can

Satanists be Satan? You betcha.

You are Satan (when you allow sin into your heart). I am Satan (when I actively work against God's plans for me).

Satan can be many. Satan can be one. Satan can be a girl. Satan can be a future person.

This idea that Satan is essentially any idea that is opposed to God need not contradict Scripture. It bears no weight on the question of angels and demons. It doesn't deny that there may be a classical Luciferian fallen angel. It doesn't deny that there can be a future, specific, personal antichrist.

Satan is the adversary to God. God has no equal, so no singular adversary can have a chance. Instead, Satan is a virus that goes from person to person, from authority to institution. We called slavery Satanic. It is. Suicidal death cults are Satanic. Any idea opposed to God: Satanic.

Satan is the adversary to God. He doesn't exist as a singular entity, but until Jesus makes all things new, he'll continue to haunt this world and claim it for his own.

Satan is the monster at the end of this book, and unless we confess our own Satan-ness to God and ask for forgiveness and healing...
We are him.

Chris' Conclusion

Our world is in physical pain from the sting of evil. That much is undeniable. As Paul rightly says in Romans, *"the whole creation is groaning together and suffering labor pains."*

What are Christians supposed to say in response to such atrocities? Where do they come from? Whose fault is it? God's? Satan's?

In short, the Biblical answer seems to be that it's our fault. We messed up. Sure, Adam and Eve had some encouragement from the snake to bite the apple, but they did it of their own will. We can pretty much sum up every evil act throughout history in the same way. We might have had some help, but ultimately we did this to ourselves and each other. Even with that knowledge, there's still one lingering question. From where did we get that help?

By our sins and actions, we are our own adversaries much of the time. Even so, we cannot discount that Scripture does point to another adversary; a third party, if you will. Neither God nor man.

This is best seen in the words of Jesus. In John 8:44, Jesus clearly shows us Satan, whoever he is, is a single entity:

Your father is the devil.

You are his children, and you want to
do what your father wants.
He was a murderer from the beginning.
He has never stood for the truth,
because there's no truth in him.
Whenever that liar speaks, he speaks
according to his own nature,
because he's a liar and the father of liars.
John 8:44 CEB

Jesus is contrasting the Pharisees' claim of Abraham as their spiritual father with the actions of one individual. The devil in this context is understood as a single entity. Jesus says *he* was a murderer and a liar from the beginning. Later in Luke, Jesus tells us that He "saw Satan fall from Heaven like lightning." We are left with little room to conclude anything else besides there existing a singular Satan.

Let's assume for a moment that much of Christian orthodoxy surrounding Satan is correct; he is the snake seen in the garden, he is the adversary in Job, the morning star that Jesus saw fall from Heaven, and the dragon enraged at God's people in the last days. Does that make him God's heavyweight opponent? I'd wager no.

Please stick with me for a second. We often use dualistic language in the church to describe God's relationship to Satan, but what if it's more of a love triangle. Well, a love/hate triangle. Yeah, this will get as messy as every sitcom trope from where I'm borrowing the metaphor. What if the title/phrase of "the adversary" or "the opposition" isn't Satan vs. God, so much as it is Satan vs. humanity.

There is only one instance of a war between Satan and God in the Scriptures, and a close look at it shows that might not be a perfect description of it. Revelation 12 describes a war in Heaven fought by Michael the Archangel and Satan alongside their accompanying armies. Christians have debated for centuries whether this represents an event yet to come or one that's already happened. I'm not sure it matters too much. John seems to go back and forth between telling a heavily metaphorical creation story and a nativity one. God doesn't appear to fight in this battle. Instead, it's a fight between spiritual forces. They battle it out until Satan and his army get thrown to the earth. That's when it gets interesting.

> *"Therefore, rejoice, you heavens and*
> *you who dwell in them.*
> *But oh! The horror for the earth and sea!*
> *The devil has come down to you with great rage,*
> *for he knows that he only has a short time."*
> *When the dragon saw that he had been thrown down*
> *to the earth, he chased the woman who had given*
> *birth to the male child. But the woman was given*
> *the two wings of the great eagle so that she could fly*
> *to her place in the desert. There she would be taken*
> *care of—out of the snake's reach—for a time and*

times and half a time. Then from his mouth the snake poured a river of water after the woman so that the river would sweep her away. But the earth helped the woman. The earth opened its mouth and swallowed the river that the dragon poured out of his mouth. So the dragon was furious with the woman, and he went off to make war on the rest of her children, on those who keep God's commandments and hold firmly to the witness of Jesus.
Revelation 12:12-17 CEB

I'm not going to lie, a lot is going on there. Notice, though, that Satan leaves this defeat to rage against the earth. Specifically, he chooses to chase our metaphorical Eve/Mary and attempts to harm their descendants. Reconcile this with what we know about the snake in the garden, and Revelation's retcon of that snake being Satan doesn't seem too far-fetched. The snake doesn't feel the need to attack God because the snake knows that it stands no chance against Him. So, the snake tricks the humans over whom he has much more sway.

Think too about the only scene of Satan and Jesus that we get together. In Matthew and Luke 4, Jesus is tempted in the wilderness by Satan. What is Satan doing? He's not attacking Jesus physically. Instead, he appeals to Jesus' human side. In attempting to trick Jesus into indulging His sense of hunger and pride, Satan wars not with Jesus' divinity, but with his humanity.

Now think about Job in this context. Satan, or the Adversary, approaches God with an appeal that humans only worship Him when things go right. So Satan has to be permitted by God to instigate Job. The scene's subtlety is that Satan isn't opposing God so much as he is opposing Job. His aim here isn't to dethrone the Creator, but instead, show that we humans only love what blesses us.

But there is one final scene with Satan we have barely touched on. The first story mentioned in this book, and perhaps the last to come to your mind. The grand *Law & Order* drama of Zechariah 3.

> *Then the Lord showed me the high priest Joshua,*
> *standing before the messenger from the Lord,*
> *and the Adversary was standing by*
> *his right side to accuse him.*
> Zechariah 3:1 CEB

There we have it. Joshua, the high priest, stands before God, the judge. A messenger is standing by Joshua's side, and off in the corner is our pesky red menace, ready to accuse him. From the opening line, this should tell us all we need to know about Satan. He is an accuser of humanity, the opponent of us.

Satan cannot fight God in this context because he knows it's a losing battle. Imagine an actual courtroom where the prosecutor chooses to physically assault the judge instead of pleading his case before him. It's not going to end well. So instead, Satan fights against an opponent he could conceivably win against; Joshua. Notice too what Joshua is wearing:

Joshua was wearing filthy clothes and
standing before the messenger.
Zechariah 3:3 CEB

Filthy clothes don't seem very becoming for a high priest. That's kind of the point, though. Consider that Joshua is believed to be the first high priest to serve in the reconstructed second temple. Furthermore, Scripture seems to credit him with helping spur the Israelites on to begin reconstruction too. All this made Joshua a pretty sacred guy. However, in this vision, we see the most prominent man of the day dressed in rags and being accused before God. Why? If anyone should be guiltless enough to pass God's test, it should be this guy! If Joshua can't do it, no one can!

The truth is Joshua can't do it. He acts as a stand-in for the people of Israel in this cosmic trial because even the best among them remains in filthy clothes. Satan has it made in the shade. This is a guaranteed win for him. But in true *Law & Order* fashion, the story isn't over without a twist.

And the Lord said to the Adversary:
"The Lord rebukes you, Adversary.
The Lord, the one choosing Jerusalem, rebukes you.

Is this one not a log snatched from the fire?"…
He responded to those standing before him,
"Take off his filthy clothes."
And he said to Joshua,
"Look, I have removed your guilt from you.
Put on priestly robes."
He said, "Put a clean turban upon his head."
So they put the clean turban upon his head,
and they dressed him in garments while
the Lord's messenger stood by.
Zechariah 3:2-5 CEB

The judge doesn't find the defendant guilty. Instead, he rules against the Adversary! God chooses Jerusalem and removes the guilt from Joshua!

While the vision of Zechariah has a happy ending, there's a scary truth hiding inside it. Satan can prevail against us easily. He doesn't fight God because he knows he can't win. So, he fights us instead. Adam and Eve are just the first in a line of naive humans that fall for his lies.

Enter Jesus. The walking God-man paradox. The perfect one made in imperfect flesh. God's way of winning for us, the final verdict that comes back in our favor.

See, in Jesus, God becomes a man and fights our opponent for us because we are powerless to defeat our adversary on our own. Because God is perfect, Satan is no match for Him. Thus, the dualistic problem of good vs. evil that we fall into quickly in our theology is entirely false. God is perfect and there is no match for Him. Satan, and his demons, are just created beings like us. It should be little wonder then that Scripture tells us "even demons believe and tremble."

So here we are, at the end of the book. Satan isn't the big bad wolf of the story any more than we are. Satan, a created being with free will, can choose to step outside of the will of God just like we can. Satan wages war against us, but praise is to God who has won the day on our behalf.

There is a monster here. Satan is real and wants to oppose us. But that fact doesn't negate the evil that exists in each one of us. The truth is we sell the Gospel short when we talk about it like some kind of cosmic battle of good vs. evil. We distill the message of God into a cheap *Star Wars* rip-off. Maybe that's what Satan wants, for us to think he has some power he doesn't. There is no battle because a battle implies a chance of victory on both sides.

The prosecution rests. The judge has ruled. The verdict is in.

ADDENDUM A

Demons

Dante here.

So, you caught us. We've spent 50,000+ words trying to pin down Satan, but barely glanced at his locker full of henchmen. Alright then, I'm saying uncle. Let's shuffle the board with these spiritual pawns.

This space could easily be subsumed by assessing the Greek and Hebrew words associated with demons and evil spirits. That is not a fruitless endeavor. Trying to comprehend the origins (and its ancient cultural impact) of the Greek word for demon, however, could take us another 50,000 words.

I think, if we try to assess the validity of a few hastily constructed propositions, we can plumb the depths much quicker.

These propositions are essentially a layout of our possible arrival destinations. Our definition of demons can't be everything. There are limits as to what those fellas can be. Demons are not fedoras.

Demons are not banana cream pies. Demons are not the year 1634. So then, as far as I can fathom, the following constitute the only intellectually arguable identities of demons.

1. They are fallen angels who chose to follow Satan and have been cast out of heaven.
2. They are gods.
3. They are God's pre-human family.
4. They are thoughts.
5. They are maladies, personified.
6. They are death, personified.
7. They are boogeymen, invented to scare us straight.

If you call yourself a Christian, it seems likely that you hold to the first proposition. This is the standard-bearer for what Christians generally perceive demons to be. It is the picture that Milton paints for us in Paradise Lost. The book of Revelation backs this imagery up with cacophonous scenes from a war in heaven accompanied by a descent of "a third of the stars".

20th-century media creations, such as *The Exorcist* and *The Screwtape Letters,* have cemented a view in the West that demons exist to haunt and terrorize us. They labor to undermine our good works, convince us that doing evil is good (oppression), or they take up residence in our being (possession).

The question then arises...

Why are there demons seemingly under every

bush in the New Testament, but scarcely any to be found in the Old Testament? This is almost an identical question to the one facing throughout this book: why is Satan so much more prominent in the New Testament? But while Satanic Old Testament references are few (the clearest being in Genesis, Ezekiel, Isaiah, Job, and Malachi), there is next to nothing regarding classical images of demons. Where are the Old Testament possessions and exorcisms? Where are the spirit-induced maladies?

In Acts 16, Paul and Silas meet a woman who has a "spirit of divination" and seems to possess supernatural powers because of it. Perhaps the closest OT parallel are the Egyptian priests who go toe-to-toe with Moses' Yahweh in Exodus. Yes, the priests are continually humbled by the God of Moses, but Scripture still says that they could successfully turn staffs into snakes and water into blood. A prima facie reading of the text would lead us to the assumption that these powers come from rival gods.

Okay, then... maybe Proposition 1 and Proposition 2 are diametrically opposed. Maybe the simplest and best way to understand the spiritual warfare dissonance between Old and New Testaments is to assert that the language of demons in the Old Testament is to call them gods and idols. That helps us make sense of 1 Corinthians 10:19-22 (ESV):

What do I imply then?
That food offered to idols is anything, or that an idol
is anything?
No, I imply that what pagans sacrifice
they offer to demons and not to God.
I do not want you to be participants with demons.
You cannot drink the cup of the Lord and the cup of
demons.
You cannot partake of the table of the Lord and the
table of demons.
Shall we provoke the Lord to jealousy?
Are we stronger than he?

If Props 1 and 2 fit together, then so does Proposition 3. The Genesis creation account gives us sunshine, water, earth, plants, animals, and humans. There's no accounting for angels and demons during the six days of creation. So, when do they come into being? There's the Satanic talking serpent, and Cherubim hanging out at the border of Eden by Genesis 3, so it seems like the rival angelic powers were already in play before God created the cosmos. God himself appears to imply the pre-existence of angels when he appears to Job:

"Where were you when I laid the foundation of the
earth?
Tell me, if you have understanding.
Who determined its measurements—surely you
know!
Or who stretched the line upon it?

> *On what were its bases sunk,*
> *or who laid its cornerstone,*
> *when the morning stars sang together*
> *and all the sons of God shouted for joy?"*
> Job 38:4-7 ESV

And that brings us back to this phrase, "sons of God". I won't replay my discussion on this phrase yet again, except to say that if we accept the term "sons of God" as an angelic/demonic term, then we can link demons (at least some of them) to these weirdos:

> *For if God did not spare angels when they sinned,*
> *but cast them into hell and committed them to chains*
> *of gloomy darkness to be kept until the judgment;*
> *if he did not spare the ancient world, but preserved*
> *Noah,*
> *a herald of righteousness, with seven others,*
> *when he brought a flood upon the world of the*
> *ungodly;*
> 2 Peter 2:4-5 ESV

Peter explicitly states that God has cast angels into hell. Okay, great. Those must be demons. Cool. Coolcoolcool. The mentioning of this judgment with the flood in the same sentence links these damned angels to the "Sons of God" referenced in Genesis 6 as one of the evil goings-ons just before the Flood. And by the time of Peter's writing, a whole mythological story based on these conniving angels had been passed around via the apocryphal book of Enoch.

Now, here's where things get tricky (or, perhaps, trickier)...

This hell that the angels are sent to... Peter doesn't actually say "hell" here. He uses a word that's not used anywhere else in Scripture. He uses a heavily baggaged word: Tartarus.

For those of you who shy away from Greek mythology, Tartarus is the deep, dark jail that Zeus and company send the Titans after their heavenly war. Who were the Titans? They were the gods before the gods. Why would Peter use this metaphor? Why invite comparisons between the Titans and demons? Fascinatingly, after the Greek war, Zeus allowed some of the Titans to persist on earth. Hmm...

And, sorry, I can't resist... If angels are "sons of God", then calling them members of God's family is accurate, no? That creates a fascinating family tree when we breathe in all of Paul's adoption language:

> *for in Christ Jesus you are all sons of God, through faith.*
> Galatians 3:26 ESV

Hard left turn. Why do we call liquor "spirits"? Generally speaking, our use of the word 'spirit' falls into three categories: ghosts, the third member of the Trinity, and various alcohols. Is there anything that binds these three groups together?

Consciousness.

A ghost is a person without a body. What makes a person a person (especially if they don't have a body!)? A consciousness. Zombies, then, are the opposite of ghosts. Ghosts are human consciousnesses without a body, while zombies are human bodies without consciousnesses. That's fun. Fun with monsters! Scripture says God is spirit. And what is spirit? Personality. Singularity. Wholeness without having a physical location. People drink alcohol because it changes their attitudes. Some folks become angry. Some become sleepy. Some become happy. Sometimes alcohol makes you all three at once. Alcohol is likely to shift your behavior. It alters the 'who' of you. That's why depressed folks are so likely to drink; they don't like the 'who' they are, so alcohol gives them a reprieve from that 'who-ness'.

When we speak of God the Father's essence, we say he *is* spirit. What we tend not to say is that he *is a* spirit. That little article says a lot. If God was a spirit, the implication is that he is one of many. Let's run with this idea of spirit = consciousness, and see if it holds water when we replace the term with its newfound definition.

> *You shall speak to all the skillful,*
> *whom I have filled with a [consciousness] of skill,*
> *that they make Aaron's garments to consecrate him*
> *for my priesthood.*

Exodus 28:3 ESV

and if the [consciousness] of jealousy comes over him...
Numbers 5:14a ESV

The [consciousness] of the Lord was upon him, and he judged Israel.
He went out to war, and the Lord gave Cushan-rishathaim
king of Mesopotamia into his hand.
And his hand prevailed over Cushan-rishathaim.
Judges 3:10 ESV

For the Lord has poured out upon you
a [consciousness] of deep sleep,
and has closed your eyes (the prophets),
and covered your heads (the seers).
Isaiah 29:10 ESV

For a [consciousness] of whoredom has led them astray,
and they have left their God to play the whore.
Hosea 4:12b ESV

"And on that day," declares the Lord of hosts,
"I will cut off the names of the idols from the land,
so that they shall be remembered no more.
And also I will remove from the land the prophets
and the [consciousness] of uncleanness."
Zechariah 13:2 ESV

"And if I cast out demons by Beelzebul,
by whom do your sons cast them out?

Therefore they will be your judges.
But if it is by the [consciousness] of God that I cast out
demons,
then the kingdom of God has come upon you."
Matthew 12:27 ESV

For all who are led by the [consciousness] of God are
sons of God.
For you did not receive the [consciousness] of slavery
to fall back into fear,
but you have received the [consciousness] of adoption
as sons,
by whom we cry, "Abba! Father!"
Romans 8:14-15 ESV

By this you know the [consciousness] of God:
every [consciousness] that confesses that Jesus Christ
has come in the flesh is from God,
and every [consciousness] that does not confess Jesus
is not from God.
This is the [consciousness] of the antichrist,
which you heard was coming and now is in the world
already.
1 John 4:2-4 ESV

It works pretty well. Maybe not perfectly, but I think it gets us to the same place. 'Spirit' seems to denote either a mentality, or a sort of possession, wherein God's presence is inside a person. Why then is it that when we see demons in the New Testament, they are constantly referred to as spirits? Is it simply because they are bodyless identities?

Let's start with an easy one. The parable of the empty house.

> *When the unclean spirit has gone out of a person,*
> *it passes through waterless places seeking rest, but*
> *finds none.*
> *Then it says, 'I will return to my house from which I*
> *came.'*
> *And when it comes, it finds the house empty, swept,*
> *and put in order.*
> *Then it goes and brings with it seven other spirits*
> *more evil than itself,*
> *and they enter and dwell there,*
> *and the last state of that person is worse than the*
> *first.*
> *So also will it be with this evil generation.*
> Matthew 12:43-45 ESV

This is a dark thing Jesus is telling us. If spirit=consciousness, differing spirits would differ by what they bring consciousness of. In other words, spirits bring an awareness of certain thoughts. Let's personify a thought. Jealousy. Here's Mr. Jealousy. He's big, mean, and green. Okay, so, apparently my mental image of jealousy is the Incredible Hulk. Very well. A man is obsessed with jealousy. All he can think about is his wife's potential infidelity. So, the Hulk has made his roost inside of this man's mind. Now, let's say he falls down, hits his head real hard, and gets amnesia, thus forgetting the incident that caused him to cuddle up with the Hulkster daily, nightly, and ever so rightly. Now, what will his mind dwell on? Nothing? If we apply Jesus' parable to the situation, unless the man's mind is filled with right thoughts, the Hulk will find his way back to the man, and bring worse thoughts with him. Maybe all this jealousy will lead to thoughts of revenge... I'd say that's a worse spirit, no?

Okay, sure, demons are thoughts... it's easy enough to make that case from a saying of Jesus, but what about an actual encounter with a demon-possessed person. Let's see if this still works... let's go to the mother of all demon possessions.

Jesus encounters the man possessed by the legion in the middle of a cemetery. We know two things about this demoniac when we meet him: he's ultra-strong, and he hurts himself physically. The spirits inside the man want nothing to do with Jesus. They urge Jesus, "In God's name don't torture me!" (Mark 5:7). Why does the man say, "In God's name"? That's fascinating, but we'll leave that there today. Legion begs not to be thrown into the "abyss" – a term that has reverberations of both Revelation and Enoch's Tartarus-like prison. Jesus casts the "impure spirits" into a nearby herd of pigs that promptly drown themselves.

Why do the pigs drown themselves? Maybe it's because they are filled with self-loathing, self-defeating, suicidal thoughts. The thoughts that were ravaging the man are now causing havoc in the pigs.

The story ends with the man wanting to follow Jesus, and instead being urged by Christ to "Return home and tell how much God has done for you" (Luke 8:39, ESV). Why doesn't the man get new bad thoughts? He's replaced the impure spirits with a spirit from the Lord. Perhaps. And perhaps also he was just a really strong guy. This abominable strength to break chains isn't necessarily supernatural. The text never directly leads us to that conclusion. So...

Maybe Proposition 1 is true: demons are fallen angels. Those fallen angels were worshiped as gods by the nations surrounding Israel (prop 2). In their beginning, they were created as members of God's family (prop 3). They possess and oppress humans by infesting the mind with a specific idea or thought (prop 4).

Now comes the different sort.

In Matthew 10:8, Jesus authorizes his disciples to cast out demons, but then, seven chapters later, they come across a case they can't beat. A mute and deaf boy is battered by horrific seizures. The boy's father asks the disciples to help, but they can't. Enter Jesus.

> *"You mute and deaf spirit, I command you,*
> *come out of him and never enter him again."*
> Mark 9:25 ESV

The boy is healed. The disciples are stunned. They

inquire of Jesus later why it is that they couldn't cast out the demon. Jesus states that this *kind* can only be cast out by prayer.

By that little word, *kind*, Jesus has introduced us to a new thought: different types of demons exist.

When our loved ones are sick, when the situation is out of our control, we pray. Perhaps the brokenness of the world, everything that isn't beautiful, maybe it's just a relic of depravity. Sometimes demons are evil thoughts, sometimes they're evil diseases. Calling them by a name is just a way to acknowledge that this world is broken, and it needs God to heal it. To make all things new.

But what are diseases and depressions and dark thoughts but harbingers of the ultimate bad thing: death? Near the tail end of Revelation, as John is about to finish the Bible with a final happily-ever-after, death itself is cast into the lake of fire. Death is killed. The language is almost certainly figurative. John wants to communicate to us that there will come a time when all bad things cease to be. He shows us this reality by personifying the ultimate bad thing, and ruining him. Death is ruined. Everything is made new.

As proposed in chapter nine, perhaps Satan is the personification of death, and demons are the personification of all the little deaths in this world. They are the instruments that bring about death. Maybe.

And that leaves us with our last proposition: there's no such thing as demons.

I can't objectively back this one. That's a pity. I was so close to synthesizing all seven propositions. So close. That being said, if we bust out our subjective looking glasses, I think there's a reality to proposition seven that holds more weight than props one through six combined.

God is sovereign. There is no one like God. In the end, all things will be made new by Jesus, Emmanuel.

What's the first thing that demons do when Jesus approaches? They yell out his name. Time and time again, we see this same procedure play out. It always makes me pause. Take the legion fellas that we already looked at. Their first words to Christ are, "What have you to do with me, Jesus, Son of the Most High God?" That sounds very respectful to me. Legion isn't just saying the name of Jesus, but stating one of his titles as well. That's what all the good boys and girls are supposed to do, right? Apparently, that's not right. Back in the day in the Near East, saying a name and title is something akin to claiming dominion over it. That's why exorcists are always trying to get the demon to say its name. They want the spiritual upper hand.

But here's the thing. We don't live in the Ancient Near East. We live in the 21st century, where having a name authorizes you to have an online presence and enhances your ability to create a following.

Spoiler alert for the movie *Hereditary.*

We don't learn until late in the third act that *Hereditary* is actually about a demon. That demon's name first appears in a book from the middle ages. I know this because the first thing I did after watching the movie was search the demon's name on Wikipedia. A Google Trends lookie-loo of the demon's name shows that almost no one searched online to learn about the demon before the movie came out. Naturally, for a couple months after the movie's release, searches for the demon skyrocketed. But the stunning part is, the search numbers have barely gone down since then. In fact, the numbers are stabilizing. People have kept searching for this guy at roughly the same rate since the film's release.

Paul encourages us to monitor our thoughts. He says:

> *Finally, brothers, whatever is true, whatever is honorable,*
> *whatever is just, whatever is pure, whatever is lovely,*
> *…whatever is commendable, if there is any excellence,*
> *if there is anything worthy of praise, think about these things.*
> Philippians 4:8 ESV

Now, it's hypocritical of me to tell you to not think about demons when I've essentially written an entire book on them. I'll take that hypocrisy if it allows me to end on this point...

Whatever demons are, whether they're warrior-spirits, bad thoughts, sex-mad cenobites, or actual diseases, there's one truth we can take comfort in: they're losers. What do we gain by investigating their nature? Little. Are we mastering them by learning their names? It didn't help Legion to know the name of Jesus.

Perhaps God, in His time, will share with us the stories and travails of the fallen spirits in full. For whatever reason, His scriptures don't enumerate those tales. I propose that our time is better spent trying to learn more about our infinite and loving God, than pondering the lackluster careers of the finite and hate-filled losers.

ADDENDUM B

Money

Chris here.

Growing up, my father had a quote that hung above his desk: "If you're going to eat and eat excessively, you're going to have to get up and kill something." Those words were spoken by self-proclaimed Christian financial guru Dave Ramsey.

Ramsey's quote was meant to inspire Christians to work hard so they could make money. Thousands of Christians have completed Ramsey's "Financial Peace University," which is supposed to give its students a Biblical view on money. The course preaches the merits of saving as much money as physically possible by cutting out anything viewed as a luxury. No more movie date nights or Starbucks coffee; if you want to be on the path to a rich life, you better save every penny you can.

While the devil may not literally be the money we earn, the picture Jesus paints of the wealthy is far from the goals Ramsey has set out for Christians. If you grab your Bible and flip to a random page in the Gospels, there is a high probability that you will find Jesus talking about money. What you see may disturb you. At the very least, it may make you sweat a little bit.

> *But how terrible for you who are rich,*
> *because you have already received your comfort.*
> *How terrible for you who have plenty now,*
> *because you will be hungry.*
> *How terrible for you who laugh now,*
> *because you will mourn and weep.*
> *How terrible for you when all speak well of you.*
> *Their ancestors did the same*
> *things to the false prophets.*
> Luke 6:24-26 CEB

Surely, Jesus can't be serious? Almost every major religion of his day, and ours, would say that the gods bless those who are wealthy. Those who have plenty have worked hard for it and should be celebrated, right?

> *"The kingdom of heaven is like a treasure that*
> *somebody hid in a field, which someone else*
> *found and covered up. Full of joy, the finder*
> *sold everything and bought that field."*
> *"Again, the kingdom of heaven is like a*
> *merchant in search of fine pearls. When he*
> *found one very precious pearl, he went and*
> *sold all that he owned and bought it."*
> Matthew 13:44-46 CEB

Okay, okay, that's easy to explain away. Jesus is talking in parables here, which means these stories are metaphorical. No one in their right mind would sell everything they have for a spiritual kingdom. No one is supposed to take these teachings as anything other than hyperbole and illustrative thinking...

The young man replied, "I've kept all these. What am I still missing?" Jesus said, "If you want to be complete, go, sell what you own, and give the money to the poor. Then you will have treasure in heaven. And come follow me."
Matthew 19:20-21 CEB

Oh... That's a little hard to ignore. Maybe Jesus meant it when He said no one could serve both money and God. See, the theme of giving up everything one owns to follow Jesus doesn't go away in the Gospels. Jesus leaves behind people who want to get their finances in place before following Him. He doesn't let a guy bury his dad for goodness sake. We know the disciples left their parents to follow Jesus, but it's likely Peter also left his wife behind! Zacchaeus, the tax collector, sells half of his belongings and uses the other half to repay those he's wronged four times more than he cheated them!

It's clear from the Gospels that Jesus expects His followers to have a dangerous disregard for their wallets. But, unfortunately, what is absent from His teaching about money is the "knuckle down and earn all you can so you can retire and live well" mentality that has infected our modern Christianity. The idea of saving money for later use is even rebuked.

In Luke 12, Jesus relates the story of a rich man who has a #firstworldproblem. He had a plentiful harvest but nowhere to store all the excess grain he collected. So whatever is this guy going to do? As any good businessman will tell you, he needs to build more storage and expand his empire. Then he will be able to take life easy and relax. If he makes it big enough, he may even be able to stop working altogether and start enjoying his life.

Before he can get the chance to sign off on the expansion, our story takes a dark turn. God demands his life from him that night. God seems almost to mock the poor soul too, taunting; "now who will get what you prepared for yourself?"

A few chapters later, Jesus tells the story of a rich man and a poor man who both die simultaneously. The poor man is taken to Abraham's side, while the rich man is tortured in the Scripture's most descriptive mention of hell. When the rich man asks for relief from Abraham, the response he gets is chilling; "remember that during your lifetime you received good things, whereas Lazarus received terrible things. Now Lazarus is being comforted, and you are in great pain."

Jesus' teaching on money and wealth is counterintuitive to what many leaders tell us today. The Gospel should offend the rich, but often we end up comforting their egos. The message of Ramsey and many others is that Christians should work to earn all they can and give their ten percent with a generous heart. But Jesus demands His followers give up everything for Him.

Does that mean you need to set this book down and rush out to sell all your material possessions? Maybe that is the call God is placing on your heart, but at the very least, Christians should seek to give before receiving. Perhaps we would be wise to heed the advice of 4th-century church father John Chrysostom in his work On Simple Living:

> "Do you want to honor the body of Christ? Then do not despise His nakedness. You come and attend church services dressed in the finest silks which your wardrobe contains; and it is right that you should honor Christ this way. But on your way do you pass naked beggars in the streets? It is no good to come to the Lord's table in fine silks, unless you also give clothes to the naked beggar-- because the body of that beggar is also the body of Christ... The service which we celebrate in church is a sham unless we put its symbolic meaning into practice outside its walls."

The Christian responsibility goes beyond taking care of just ourselves or our families; it extends to every person we meet. If our wealth isn't being actively given to those in more profound need, we live in the shadow of Jesus' teachings. We may even find ourselves in company with those nameless rich men who worshiped at the altar of wealth and met unfortunate ends. We are not called to eat and eat excessively, but instead, our lives should reflect the attitude towards money that John Wesley had who said we should throw money out of our hands as quickly as possible; "lest it should find its way into your heart."

Also By Chris Kaufman

Today the American evangelical church is in a crisis. Evangelical Christians make up only 25% of the population and that number is dropping all the time. Movements like the "Exvangelical" are becoming more popular in what used to be the dominant vein of Christianity. Those outside the Evangelical church see us as judgmental, hypocritical, and angry and not without good reason. Many Christians can quote John 3:16 from memory, but few are as familiar with the rest of Jesus' life and teachings. Amidst an ever-growing political divide in the country and the church, we need to again ask ourselves, what does it mean to follow the Jesus revealed in the Gospels in this Empire? Join Chris on this journey through the life of Jesus in the first century. Uncover with him the responsibilities of modern Christians in America. Sit in the tension of life in the Empire and the Kingdom and laugh at the terrible jokes along the way. What you learn may just surprise you.

And Don't Forget About...

The Epic of Gilgamesh is the oldest story ever preserved. What's it about? What can it tell us about humanity? How similar is King Gilgamesh of Uruk to the modern man? What can we learn from history's first warrior king?

Dante walks us through the ancient story tablet by tablet, delightfully integrating pop culture references into his retelling. While Dante's tone is fresh and witty, a dark question haunts the pages of his 'ancient book review': does the Epic of Gilgamesh tell us anything about the God of the Bible? Is it possible the Bible stole from the Sumerian tradition? The answers may have dramatic consequences for all of us.

Come for the history lesson.
Stay for the jokes.